WHAT THE CRITICS SAY:

A very worthwhile addition to any travel library.
　　　　　　　　　　　　　　　　　　　　　　—WCBS Newsradio

Armed with these guides, you may never again stay in a conventional hotel.
　　　　　　　　　　　　　　　　　　　　　　—Travelore Report

Easily carried ... neatly organized ... wonderful. A helpful addition to my travel library. The authors wax as enthusiastically as I do about the almost too-quaint-to-believe Country Inns.　　　　　**—San Francisco Chronicle**

One can only welcome such guide books and wish them long, happy, and healthy lives in print.　　　　　　　　　　　　　　**—Wichita Kansas Eagle**

This series of pocket-sized paperbacks will guide travelers to hundreds of little known and out of the way inns, lodges, and historic hotels.... a thorough menu.
　　　　　　　　　　　　　　—(House Beautiful's) Colonial Homes

Charming, extremely informative, clear and easy to read; excellent travelling companions.　　　　　**—Books-Across-The-Sea** *(The English Speaking Union)*

...a fine selection of inviting places to stay... provide excellent guidance....
　　　　　　　　　　　　　　—Blair & Ketchum's Country Journal

Obviously designed for our kind of travel.... [the authors] have our kind of taste.
　　　　　　　　　　　　　　　　　　　　　　—Daily Oklahoman

The first guidebook was so successful that they have now taken on the whole nation.... Inns are chosen for charm, architectural style, location, furnishings and history.　　　　　　　　　　　　　　**—Portland Oregonian**

Many quaint and comfy country inns throughout the United States... The authors have a grasp of history and legend.　　　　　**—Dallas (Tx.) News**

Very fine travel guides.　　　　　　　　**—Santa Ana (Calif.) Register**

A wonderful source for planning trips.　　　**—Northampton (Mass.) Gazette**

...pocketsize books full of facts.... attractively made and illustrated.
　　　　　　　　　　　　　　　　—New York Times Book Review

Hundreds of lovely country inns reflecting the charm and hospitality of various areas throughout the U.S.　　　　　　　**—Youngstown (Ohio) Vindicator**

Some genius must have measured the average American dashboard, because the Compleat Traveler's Companions fit right between the tissues and bananas on our last trip.... These are good-looking books with good-looking photographs.... very useful.

　　　　　　　　　　　　　　　　—East Hampton (N.Y.) Star

ALSO AVAILABLE IN THE COMPLEAT TRAVELER SERIES

If your local bookseller, gift shop, or country inn does not stock a particular title, ask them to order directly from Burt Franklin & Co., Inc., 235 East 44th Street, New York, 10017, U.S.A. Telephone orders are accepted from recognized retailers and credit-card holders. In the U.S.A., call, toll-free, 1-800-223-0766 during regular business hours. (In New York State, call 212-687-5250.)

COUNTRY INNS

Lodges, and Historic Hotels of the

SOUTH

by

Anthony Hitchcock

and

Jean Lindgren

BURT FRANKLIN & COMPANY

Published by
BURT FRANKLIN & COMPANY
235 East Forty-fourth Street
New York, New York 10017

SEVENTH EDITION

Library of Congress Cataloging in Publication Data

Hitchcock, Anthony
Country inns, lodges, and historic hotels
of the South.
(The Compleat traveler's companion).
Includes index.
1. Hotels, taverns, etc. — Southern States — Directories.
I. Lindgren, Jean, joint author. II. Title. III. Series:
Compleat traveler's companion
TX907.H5396   1985   647'.947'501
ISBN 0-89102-311-9 (pbk.)

Cover Illustration courtesy of
The Battery Carriage House
Charleston, South Carolina

Manufactured in the United States of America

Published simultaneously in Canada by
FITZHENRY & WHITESIDE
195 Allstate Parkway
Markham, Ontario L3R 4T8

3 4 2

Contents

Introduction

FOR MANY YEARS the South meant for us the drive down the coastal highways in the late winter, just as we could no longer bear another day of Northern slush and drizzle. The magic of the South then meant watching nature emerge from its winter shrouds as every hour of driving brought us closer to our Southern goal. The first hint of jasmine or silver-gray Spanish moss meant we were really there. If we were not impatient, we would stop fleetingly in Williamsburg or another of the more northerly cities of the South. But, in truth, the thought of Florida's golden sunshine and fresh-picked fruit drove us relentlessly on.

Looking back, we feel it is a shame to have missed most of the South in those nearly annual pilgrimages. To linger in the Great Smoky Mountains or paddle along a Louisiana bayou is just a hint of the pleasures to come. Texas, for example, is truly a land of contrasts, with pleasures unimagined by the coastbound traveler. The interstate superhighways, with their ability to change a region's character in the interests of speed and convenience, led us around the great cities of Savannah and Charleston. Slow down and plan to linger awhile to savor the true Southern hospitality that extends throughout this great region.

The South is slow and easy, filled with history, beauty, and fine home cooking. And it is now, more than ever, for all four seasons. More and more the mid-South inns are remaining open the year round to welcome visitors: some facilities do close in the winter months, but a call to your innkeeper should confirm which ones will be open.

We also suggest you write early for literature about inns that you have chosen as interesting. Read the brochures, look at the pictures, check the maps, and determine if the inns will actually meet your needs. Inns are not at all like motels. Each has its special qualities that may appeal to one person but not to another. Do not hesitate to call an innkeeper and discuss your requirements. In fact, we feel that this is, for us, the most important thing to do before making a reservation. Country inns reflect the style and personality of the innkeeper. This personal ambience is more likely to affect your visit than in a motel or large hotel. Most innkeepers are highly understanding of the needs of their guests. If you are seeking, for example, an old-fashioned small country inn that is secluded from most outside distractions, ask before you go. We have purposely included a wide range of inns, lodges, small and historic hotels, and small resorts.

We have quoted the most recent room rates in a combined rate chart and index at the end of the book. Readers should note that the listed rates are *subject to change*. While the quoted rates are for double occupancy in most cases, single travelers as well as larger groups should inquire about special rates. We list daily room rates as based on the American Plan (AP, all three meals included), Modified American Plan (MAP, breakfast and dinner included), Bed and Breakfast (BB, full or Continental breakfast included), or European Plan (EP, no meals). In many cases a tax and a service charge will be added. Be sure to ask. Children and pets present special problems for many inns. If either is *not* welcome at an inn, it is noted in the description. These regulations also often change, and it is imperative that families traveling with either inquire in advance. Even though many inns state that they are open all year, we find that many of these close spontaneously during slow periods. Call first to confirm your room reservations.

We suggest that before traveling to any state you write to its department of travel and tourism. Ask for the state road map and a packet of general travel information. If you have special travel interests or needs, the department can often send special pamphlets or hints. In the pages that follow, readers will discover that the material is organized by state. Within each state, listings are alphabetical by the names of the towns and villages. For those seeking a particular inn, there is an index at the end of the book, which also contains rate and credit-card information.

The inns discussed in this book were chosen for their inherent charm, based partially on their architectural style, location, furnishings, and history. We used no strict definition of an "inn" in selecting places for inclusion. Although the term usually denotes a place with both lodging and food, we have listed several that provide no meals. We find, in some cases, that the food operation actually is so dominant as to detract from the quiet and charm of a place. We did not include any of the old inns that only serve meals, although a great many exist in the region. We have made every effort to provide information as carefully and accurately as possible, but we remind readers again that all rates and schedules are subject to change. Finally, we have neither solicited nor accepted any fees or gratuities for inclusion of an inn in this book or in any other book in the Compleat Traveler series.

We would like this book to continue to grow in usefulness in succeeding editions. We very much wish to hear of your experiences at the inns listed in this volume and to receive your suggestions for future volumes. We will make every effort to answer all letters personally. Please write to us in care of our publishers: Burt Franklin & Co., 235 East Forty-fourth Street, New York, NY 10017.

Have a good trip!

JEAN LINDGREN
ANTHONY HITCHCOCK

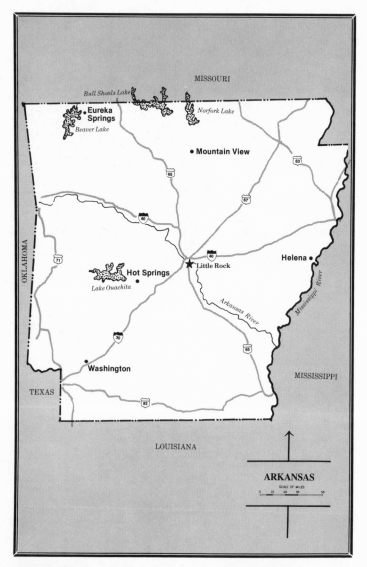

MISSOURI

Bull Shoals Lake

Norfork Lake

Eureka
Springs

Beaver Lake

● Mountain View

OKLAHOMA

Hot Springs

Lake Ouachita

★ Little Rock

Helena ●

Arkansas River

Mississippi River

Washington

TEXAS

MISSISSIPPI

LOUISIANA

ARKANSAS

SCALE OF MILES

0   10   20   30   40   50

Arkansas

Eureka Springs, Arkansas

CRESCENT COTTAGE INN

211 Spring Street, Eureka Springs, AR 72632. 501-253-6022. *Innkeepers:* Ron and Brenda Bell. Open April through December.

The whole town of Eureka Springs is a festival of Victorian architecture, and Crescent Cottage is no exception. Located in the historic residential section of town, it was built in 1881 by Arkansas' first Governor, Powell Clayton. Today Crescent Cottage, authentically painted in the colorful Victorian tradition, offers good views of the surrounding green mountains and hollows. In the distance, the statue of Christ can be seen in its setting for the Passion Play, performed each year in the neighboring hills. The inn's back yard has a flower garden designed to provide blooms all summer long. The cottage is decorated with Victorian country antiques and period wallpapers. Quilts top antique oak or painted scrolly iron beds. Breakfast is served in the dining room and is a good time to discuss the day's plans with Ron and Brenda, whose knowledge of the area make them ideal consultants. The inn is within walking distance of shops and restaurants.

Accommodations: 5 rooms, 1 with private bath. *Pets and children:* Not permitted. *Driving Instructions:* The inn is on Route 62B in downtown Eureka Springs.

CRESCENT HOTEL

75 Prospect Street, Eureka Springs, AR 72632. 501-253-9766. *Innkeeper:* Jerry Hope. Open all year.

The Crescent Hotel's brochure reads, "For a trip to the Victorian world of 1886 come to the Crescent." The old Gothic hotel with its high turrets and towering brick chimneys is set on the crest of the Ozarks' West Mountain overlooking the winding streets and gingerbread houses of Eureka Springs. The Crescent Hotel was originally built to house the thousands of people flocking to the springs to partake of the healing mineral waters. Some of the 27 acres of rugged woodland surrounding the Crescent have been landscaped to include shaded lawns, flagstone walks, and a swimming pool. Four stories of balconies are supported by tall white columns.

At the turn of the century, the resort business took a definite turn for the worse, and the Crescent closed its doors for most of each year. During the Depression, the hotel fell into the hands of a disreputable and colorful (literally and figuratively) character who painted the entire place orchid to match his clothes, car, and stationery. He operated an unusual hospital in the hotel from behind a bulletproof shield on his octagonal desk in the Governor's Suite. He kept loaded tommy guns and had a secret escape route to the roof, but he was eventually arrested and imprisoned for fraud.

A group of interested partners took over the hotel in the late 1940s, and the entire place was then totally restored. Victorian furnishings were found to replace those lost or damaged over the years, and once again the rooms were filled with rugs, drapes, furniture, and fixtures of the opulent, bygone Golden Age. Today the hotel has several striking public rooms and seventy-six guest rooms and suites. The rooms are furnished with the period antiques and reproductions. There are velvet-covered walnut or mahogany carved lounges and chairs, marble-topped tables, and brass or carved wooden beds. The lighting is a combination of crystal or brass chandeliers and old converted oil lamps. Many of the rooms open onto airy balconies overlooking the town and forests, while others have sunny alcoves with views of the lawns.

On the hotel's rooftop is the "Top of the Crescent" lounge, where guests can sip cocktails in the Victorian elegance of a sea of white wicker and mirrors. Down in the Crystal Dining Room, guests and the

public dine in a room with polished bare floors, a wall of tall, graceful windows, red velvet wall panels, and lit by crystal chandeliers. Large marble-topped sideboards line the sides of the room.

Accommodations: 76 rooms with private bath. *Pets:* Only a few well-behaved pets are permitted; check first. *Driving Instructions:* In Eureka Springs, take Route 62B to the hotel door.

DAIRY HOLLOW HOUSE

Dairy Hollow Road, Eureka Springs, Arkansas. Mailing address: P.O. Box 221, Eureka Springs, AR 72632. 501-253-7444. *Innkeepers:* Crescent Dragonwagon, Ned Shank, Amrit and Mark Realyea. Open all year.

Dairy Hollow House clings to a mountain slope in a secluded valley just minutes from Eureka Springs. The inn has been renovated to display a gracious style unheard of in the nineteenth century, when it was built as an Ozark dairy farm's farmhouse. As tiny as Dairy Hollow House is, it has grown in stages. Its history began in 1889, when Daniel McIntyre built the first room. A second room was added the next year; and the final one, in 1925. The three-room farmhouse remained in the McIntyre family until the time of the death of its previous owner, when Dairy Hollow was the last small dairy farm operating in Eureka Springs.

For many years Ned Shank, president of the Eureka Springs Preservation Society, and his wife had longed to purchase the aging farmhouse. With the help of singer-songwriter Bill Haymes they did so in 1977 and set out on their ambitious renovation. At first alone and later with the help of a number of Eureka Springs craftsmen, the innkeepers stripped paint and wallpaper, hand-planed wainscoting, installed etched and stained-glass windows, refinished antique furniture, and commissioned hand quilting for the beds.

One enters Dairy Hollow House through a landscaped garden that is brilliant with blooms throughout the warmer months. After crossing a traditional "set a spell" porch, one enters the parlor–breakfast room, with its original wood paneling now gleaming because of its careful restoration by the innkeepers. This room is trimmed in reds — red patchwork pillows on the floor and red calico curtains at the windows. An ornate wood stove stands on a brick hearth in the parlor, adding its warmth to the building's central heating in the cooler months. The stained-glass window in this room was made by a local craftsman. It is here that the inn's very special breakfasts are served. Crescent, author of several cookbooks, oversees the menus. The innkeepers provide "rave review" dinners for overnight guests, by advance arrangement.

One of the guest rooms, the Rose Room, has a double bed covered with a Dutch-rose handmade quilt. This pattern, also called captive beauty, was made by a local woman who quilts in her own home. The

Rose Room has an Eastlake-style "gentleman's bureau" topped with marble, a cherry night table, and antique hand-hooked rugs. The Rose Room's bathroom has a big old claw-footed tub and a large skylight.

The other guest room, the Iris Room, entered from the porch, is done in shades of blue and contains quilt-covered twin beds. The quilt patterns here are called bear's paw and goose tracks. An antique bureau and night tables match the oaken framing on the iris-patterned etched-glass window. The shades in this room, as well as those in the Rose Room, were handwoven by a Eureka Springs craftsman. The combined artistry of many local men and women is one of the things that make a stay at Dairy Hollow House so pleasant.

Accommodations: 2 rooms with private bath. *Pets:* Not permitted. *Children:* Under 10 not permitted. *Driving Instructions:* Take Route 62 (Spring Street) past Grotto Spring Cave. Turn right at the sign for the inn, and follow the arrows.

NEW ORLEANS HOTEL

63 Spring Street, Eureka Springs, AR 72632. 501-253-8630. Open all year.

When it was built in 1882, the New Orleans Hotel was called the Wadsworth. Constructed to accommodate some of the crowds pouring into Eureka Springs to enjoy its health spas, the Wadsworth soon changed its name, first to the Alfred Hotel and then to the Springs. It carried the latter name until 1951 when, because of the elaborate wrought-iron work on the second- and third-floor balconies, it was given its current name. During the 1950s and 1960s, the New Orleans underwent "modernization" that included installation of acoustical drop ceilings, wall paneling, and shag carpeting. Today most of the "improvements" have been removed, and the hotel is listed in the National Register of Historic Places.

An indicator of the success of the restoration was the choice of the hotel for a number of interior scenes in *Belle Starr*, a movie made for public television. The movie company was taken with the lobby, staircases, and restored rooms, and it shot several scenes in them. On entering the lobby, it is easy to see why the movie producers chose the New Orleans Hotel. The spacious room has tall, tin-roofed ceilings, a handsome registration desk and old-fashioned cash register, tall paneled four-square columns supporting the ceiling, and wainscoting rising part way up the walls to meet the bold Victorian wallpaper. At the head of the stairs on each of the upper three floors are smaller guest lobbies that have Victorian touches, such as ponderous old high-back mirrored bench chairs, Oriental area rugs, and small tables.

Each guest room is different, and although the Victorian feeling predominates, a few earlier pieces may be found. Some rooms still have to be restored, and not all furnishings are antique, but that is the direction in which the hotel is heading.

The hotel's restaurant has no menu; the bill of fare is written on blackboards. Recent luncheon specials included ham steak, sweet potatoes, and salad, and honey-baked chicken, corn-bread dressing, and cole slaw. Breakfast is also served here. At the underground level of the hotel is another restaurant, called "The Quarter." It has its own cocktail lounge.

Accommodations: 24 rooms, 18 with private bath and 6 with connecting bath. *Driving Instructions:* Take Route 16B into town, where it becomes Spring Street. The hotel is there, in the historic district.

Helena, Arkansas

EDWARDIAN INN

317 Briscoe Street, Helena, AR 72342. 501-338-9155. *Innkeepers:* Mac and Joan McGinty. Open all year.

The crescendo of interest in bed and breakfast has been a boon to the traveling public and innkeepers, as well as the salvation of many a grand, but formerly neglected, historic home or mansion. The Edwardian is a perfect example. Built by a wealthy cotton broker in 1901, no expense was spared in creating one of the most elaborate homes of its time in Arkansas. Well over $100,000 later, the broker was bankrupt, and the beautiful building fell into disrepair. Slated for demolition, it was rescued by investors and transformed into an inn, recapturing the elegance of the Edwardian era.

The rooms have period antiques set against a backdrop of exquisite woodwork, beveled glass mirrors, crystal chandeliers, and tiled and carved mantle, enhanced by the convenience of modern baths, television, central air-conditioning, and ceiling fans. The inn has unusual floors—a wood parquet "carpet" that was created in Germany, applied to canvas backing, rolled up, shipped to Helena, and installed in the house. Breakfast is served in the latticed sun room, while guests enjoy relaxing in the sitting room in the upper hall. A honeymoon suite on the third floor offers views of the Mississippi River.

Accommodations: 12 rooms with private bath. *Driving Instructions:* The inn is 60 miles souuth of Memphis on the Mississippi River.

Hot Springs National Park, Arkansas

WILLIAMS HOUSE

420 Quapaw, Hot Springs National Park, AR 71901. 501-624-4275. *Innkeepers:* Mary and Gary Riley. Open all year.

Mary and Gary Riley have put a great deal of time, energy, and enthusiasm into their inn and take very seriously the business of "bed and breakfast," emphasizing just that — good beds (they had them custom-made) and good breakfast (choices vary daily, with eggs Benedict, eggs fricassee, omelets, waffles, grits, and baked toast amandine appearing regularly).

Williams House is an elaborate Victorian structure built in 1890 and now listed in the National Register of Historic Places. It retains many of its original features and is considered unusual in the area because of its brick and brownstone construction. The building has a wraparound porch and even a stone tower.

Inside, oak and walnut pocket-doors have stained-glass and beveled-glass windows. The woodwork is impressive, with paneled wainscoting in some rooms. The inn is furnished throughout with Victorian antiques and has many antique lighting fixtures. A baby grand piano has a welcoming position by the front door in the sunny entrance hall, which is furnished with a camel-backed sofa and Victorian side chairs. The 12-foot-high ceilings accommodate a towering beveled mirror in the parlor. The atmosphere is most relaxing, with plenty of houseplants in nooks and on fanciful carved oaken and walnut antiques.

Each guest room has its own personality and special touches. The Parlor Suite has beautiful walnut woodwork, a brass bed, and, in its private bathroom, a marble shower and antique pedestal sink. The Front Chamber has an unusual imported French marble sink, with flowers painted on it, and a heavy oaken bedstead, lengthened for comfort. One room has a porch, and another overlooks the garden. Several of the antique-filled rooms can be combined to form suites for families or couples traveling together. The carriage house has two more informal guest rooms with country antiques.

Williams House is just four blocks from Bathhouse Row and the convention and visitors' center. Hot Springs, renowned for its mineral baths, was the first United States national park. Although the area surrounding Hot Springs is quite beautiful, the town itself has attracted a number of amusement parks, restaurants, and giant motel-hotel complexes. Williams House allows guests to escape from all that while still having it close at hand. The town is on Lake Ouachita, known for its undeveloped shoreline and picturesque islands.

Accommodations: 5 rooms, 3 with private bath. *Pets and Preschool Children:* Not permitted. *Driving Instructions:* Take Routes 7, 70, or 270 to Hot Springs.

Mountain View, Arkansas

THE INN AT MOUNTAIN VIEW

Route 5, Mountain View, Arkansas. Mailing address: P.O. Box 812, Mountain View, AR 72560. 501-269-4200. *Innkeeper:* Larraine Leddy. Open all year.

Mountain View, the folk capital of the Ozarks, has Saturday-night hootenannies and other folk-music programs throughout the summer. The town and inn sit in the heart of the Ozark Mountains amid hill-country scenery. The inn, built in 1886, is furnished with Victorian antiques and Oriental rugs on dark-stained pine-board floors. The guest suites upstairs are furnished with period pieces. Guests have use of the parlor and the living room, with its old-fashioned stone fireplace, and rockers line the veranda, where guests can catch the evening breezes. Country breakfasts are served in the breakfast room. The Ozark Folk Center is nearby, as is the Grandpa Jones Family Dinner Theater. The surrounding mountains are perfect for hiking and horseback riding. Larraine will steer interested guests to local canoeing and fishing spots.

Accommodations: 9 suites with private bath. *Pets:* Not permitted. *Driving Instructions:* The inn is a two-hour drive north of Little Rock on Route 5.

THE OLD COUNTY JAIL

State Highway 4, Washington, AR 71862. 501-983-2178. *Innkeeper:* Mrs. J. B. Summers. Open all year.

More than a century ago Washington, Arkansas, was a staging point for Americans setting out on the Great Southwest Trail to the Western Frontier. Sam Houston stopped here to plot the liberation of Texas, and the first Bowie knife was shaped in Washington. Antebellum homes, the old tavern, a museum, and a pioneer cemetery are a part of this restored historic pioneer town now operated as part of the state park system. Recently the old Washington jail was purchased by innkeeper J. B. Summers and refurbished to contain guest rooms and a restaurant.

All furnishings in the Old County Jail date from the last half of the nineteenth century. The inn's exterior is painted a crisp white with black trim. Its rooms have been painstakingly restored and decorated; a music-and-game room complete with grand piano and an inlaid game table is for the use of overnight guests. There is a fireplace in the formal parlor, and outside, rockers line the galleries.

J. B. prepares special dinners each evening. No set menu is used, but typical entrées include prime ribs, seafood, pork, lamb, game hens, and duck. Guests should note that the inn is in a dry county, so they should bring their own alcoholic beverages, if they wish.

Accommodations: 7 rooms with private bath. *Pets:* Not permitted. *Children:* Permitted for dining only. *Driving Instructions:* The state park is on State Highway 4, north of Hope.

Florida

THE BAILEY HOUSE

28 South Seventh Street, Box 805, Fernandina Beach, FL 32034. 904-261-5390. *Innkeepers:* Tom and Diane Hay. Open all year.

Amelia Island stretches for 13 miles just south of Cumberland Island, off the northern Atlantic coast of Florida. Fernandina Beach is the largest village on the island and the home of The Bailey House, a Queen Anne-style bed-and-breakfast inn built in 1895. Designed by George Barber of Knoxville, the building has turrets, gables, bay windows, and fish-scale decorative shinglework. The house was built by steamship company agent Effingham Bailey for his bride, and much of its fine detailed woodwork was probably executed by skilled boatbuilders.

Bailey House has six fireplaces including the largest, in the reception hall, which bears the inscription "Hearth Hall–Welcome All." In the dining room and parlor, both open to guests, are a number of antique pieces including an old pump organ that guests enjoy using. All bedrooms have private period baths with claw-footed tubs as well as separate tiled showers, pedestal sinks, and oaken toilets. Two of the larger rooms have fireplaces. The Rose Room is the most elegant and includes a large sitting area in a turret. Guests enjoy the front

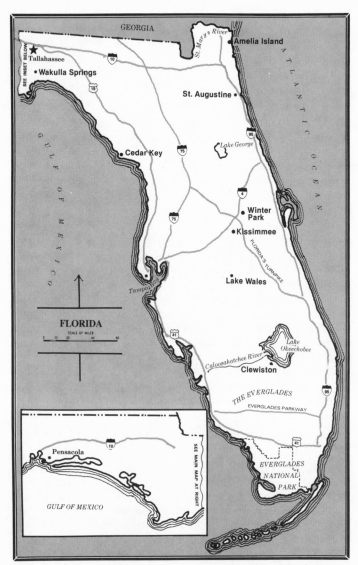

porch with its old porch swing and wicker rockers. This is the only spot at Bailey House where smoking is permitted. A Continental breakfast is served to guests.

Accommodations: 4 rooms with private bath. *Pets:* Not permitted. *Children:* Under ten not permitted. *Driving Instructions:* From I-95, take Route A1A to Amelia Island. Take a left on Center Street and another left onto Seventh Street.

THE 1735 HOUSE

584 South Fletcher Avenue, Amelia Island, FL 32034. 904-261-5878. *Innkeepers:* David and Susan Caples. Open all year.

In 1735, Governor James Olglethorpe of Georgia, while on an expedition, marveled at the beauty of a barrier island his party had discovered. He later named the island Amelia, in honor of King George II's sister. Although it was constructed in 1928, The 1735 House takes its name from this significant date in the island's history.

The 1735 House is the only country inn in Florida that directly faces the Atlantic Ocean. The Cape Cod–style frame house is painted white with black shutters. Each guest room is set up like a suite, with an antique-furnished bedroom on the building's street side, a captain's bunk-bed area in the center of the room, and a living room facing the surf. A romantic lighthouse is a favorite with guests.

Breakfast, delivered to the guest rooms in wicker baskets, includes breakfast rolls, juice, fresh fruit, and coffee or tea. The inn overlooks a quiet, undisturbed section of Amelia's 13-mile stretch of beach. It is about 2 miles from the harbor area with its shops and restaurants.

Accommodations: 6 suites with private bath. *Pets:* Not permitted. *Driving Instructions:* From I-95, exit at Yulee, Florida. Go east on A1A to Amelia Island, where A1A becomes South Fletcher Avenue.

ISLAND HOTEL

Main Street, Cedar Key, FL 32625. 904-543-5111. *Innkeeper:* Marcia Rogers. Open all year except January.

The Island Hotel, built in 1850, was occupied during the Civil War by soldiers from both the Confederate and Union armies. Cedar Key is a small community on the sandy island known as Way Key. About 150 miles north of Saint Petersburg, Way is the only occupied island of a group of about forty that dot the Gulf of Mexico coastline. Since World War II Cedar Key has enjoyed a gradual revitalization, although it remains a sleepy fishing town, a sort of living museum of Florida coastal life half a century ago.

The Island Hotel is a galleried two-story building whose exterior is covered with tabby, the blend of crushed oystershell and limestone used extensively in northern Florida. The inn's lobby summons up memories of Casablanca with its slowly turning ceiling fans, potbelly stove, and two parrots standing proudly on a perch. Double French doors lead to a dining veranda, and classical music fills the air.

The inn's chef prepares shark "Island Hotel," soft-shell crabs with lemon butter, trout with dill sauce, and scallops Provençale. Grouper and redfish come in several guises, and stone crabs and oysters are served on occasion. Pecan pie is a favorite dessert. Murals in the King Neptune Lounge depict Cedar Key scenes. The room's "sunset" deck is a nice place to meet local fishermen and listen to their tales.

Guest rooms, upstairs off a parlor with murals, are simply furnished with a bureau, beds, and a side table. On weekends, the bar downstairs is usually full, as is the veranda, which makes for a very lively crowd — be prepared to join the activities until late in the evening. The upstairs veranda is furnished with a hammock for two, a swing, and oak rockers. Breakfast offerings include pancakes with cranberry-apple topping, bacon and eggs, and grits and potatoes.

Accommodations: 10 rooms, 3 with private bath. *Pets:* Permitted for a fee. *Driving Instructions:* Take Route 24 west to Cedar Key. Turn left on Main Street to the inn.

Clewiston, Florida

CLEWISTON INN

U.S. 27 and 108 Royal Palm Avenue, Clewiston, Florida. Mailing address: P.O. Drawer 1297, Clewiston, FL 33440. 813-983-8151. *Innkeeper:* Betty Hill, Manager. Open all year.

The Clewiston Inn is a white brick building with large, crescent-topped, full-story windows and a portico supported by four tall, square columns, built fewer than fifty years ago. The public rooms have beamed ceilings, built-in china-display cabinets, tongue-and-groove pine paneling, and fireplaces. The lobby has a handsome, old-fashioned look, with several couches grouped around the fireplace. Outside are manicured lawns dotted with palm and other semitropical trees and shrubs. The guest rooms are decorated with reproduction Spanish Provincial furniture.

The dining room at the Clewiston now serves only a daily buffet dinner that includes choices of roast beef, baked ham, roast pork, baked fish, lamb, chops of some sort, and boneless stuffed chicken. The meats are accompanied by fourteen salads and several choices of potatoes, beans, and vegetables. The buffet is available at lunch and dinner. Breakfast from a standard menu is also available.

Accommodations: 56 rooms with private bath. *Driving Instructions:* Take Route 27 directly into Clewiston.

THE BEAUMONT HOUSE, BED AND BREAKFAST

206 South Beaumont Avenue, Kissimmee, FL 32741. 305-846-7916. *Innkeepers:* Rudell and Gerald Kopp. Open all year.

Kissimmee is an old-fashioned Florida town on Lake Tohopekaliga. Strolling the quiet palm- and live oak-lined streets, one is just minutes away from the bustle of Florida's main tourist attractions — Epcot, Disney World, Sea World, Circus World, and Reptile World.

Rudell and Gerald Kopp have restored their Victorian home, built in 1905 on a corner lot surrounded by trees. A lone grapefruit tree shares the back yard with the swimming pool, one of the Kopp's few concessions to modern amenities. The centerpiece of the Victorian parlor is an ornate circular staircase that leads to a balcony and the innkeeper's quarters. Cooled by a paddle fan, the parlor has lace curtains, leaded-glass windows, and solid, no-frills Victorian furnishings that create an unusually authentic atmosphere. The four guest rooms are also furnished with period antiques set off by ornate flower and stripe wallpapers. Two rooms have private entrances from the veranda, as well as mahogany fireplace mantels. Antique quilts are on Victorian beds, while matching accessories enhance the atmosphere.

The Kopps are avid collectors of Victoriana, and most items are for sale. If you take a fancy to that handsome walnut burl bed or Victorian lady's chair, it can be yours. In the morning, breakfast is served in the parlor.

Accommodations: 4 rooms with shared baths. *Pets:* Not permitted. *Driving Instructions:* From the intersection of Routes 444 and 192, take Route 17/92 south. Bear right on Broadway and then take Emmett Street to Beaumont Avenue. Turn left on Beaumont and drive two blocks to the inn.

Lake Wales, Florida

CHALET SUZANNE INN AND RESTAURANT

U.S. 27 and 17A, Lake Wales, Florida. Mailing address: P.O. Box AC, Lake Wales, FL 33853. 813-676-6011. *Innkeepers:* Carl and Vita Hinshaw. Open all year, except Mondays June through November.

Some inns are done in Early American, some in French Provincial, others in late Victorian. Chalet Suzanne is done in dazzling eclectic. This fairy-tale assemblage of buildings is a testimony to one woman's zeal for living. In the 1920s Carl Hinshaw, Sr., and his wife, Bertha, left Chicago for the warmer climes of Florida. Carl, Sr., passed away, leaving Bertha with only their home, a car, and two children in the middle of the Depression, in the middle of Florida. Undeterred, Bertha took stock of her assets and realized that her years of travel and entertaining had given her an eccentric but solid training for running a restaurant. The Hinshaws went up and down the highway announcing "Chalet Suzanne," named after a daughter. After ten days, a family of four from Miami arrived and stayed two weeks, and that was the beginning of a lifelong tradition of innkeeping.

Chalet Suzanne is a grouping of interconnected buildings reminiscent of a "Moorish-Bavarian" town. Towers, turrets, and minarets are the rule, and stone and stucco blend with wood-shingled "witch's-hat" roofs. There are tile tables in the Swiss dining room, and bathrooms with tiled walls, tiled floors, and tiled, custom-made bathtubs.

The air-conditioned rooms have overstuffed furniture, lacquered tables, parquet floors, imported patterned carpeting, rough plastered walls, porcelain lamps, massive four-poster beds, telephones, and hand-painted tiles. Even the gates to the estate came from foreign lands.

Chalet Suzanne's excellence is perhaps clearest in the dining rooms, which reflect the inn's birth as an eating establishment. As such, it garners awards year after year. The restaurant's stained-glass windows, tiled floors and walls, warm wooden ceilings, and place settings all set the atmosphere. The china collection is extensive, and fresh flowers abound here as they do throughout the inn.

Chalet Suzanne's soups are so popular that they are sold in gourmet shops across the country and in Europe. Dinner entrées include chicken Suzanne topped with an amber glaze, lobster Newburg, lump crabmeat in herb butter, king crab Thermidor, curried shrimp, lamb chops, and filet mignon with béarnaise sauce.

Accommodations: 30 rooms with private bath. *Driving Instructions:* Take either U.S. 27 or Route 60 to Lake Wales. The inn is 4½ miles north of town, on U.S. 27 and Route 17A.

St. Augustine, Florida

CASA DE SOLANA

21 Aviles Street, St. Augustine, FL 32084. 904-824-3555. *Innkeepers:* Jim and Faye McMurry. Open all year.

Casa de Solana is a renovated Colonial home built around 1763. The exact date of construction is unknown, but the house is on a 1764 map of St. Augustine. The cocquina structure, with its carriage house and private courtyard, still has its original hand-hewn beams, pegged flooring, and moldings. The house, in the heart of St. Augustine's picturesque historic district, was transformed into a country inn by the McMurrys, who live on the second floor, where guests are invited to join them for wine and cheese in their living room. The rooms in the inn are furnished with the McMurrys' collection of English antiques. Some of the guest rooms are in the attached carriage house; others are in the main house. An attic suite has sloping eaves and a chimney through the middle of the room. The most lavish of the rooms is the Bridal Suite in the carriage house.

A full Southern breakfast is served in the formal dining room, which has a crystal chandelier and a 10-foot mahogany table on a lush Oriental carpet. If guests prefer, they can have breakfast out on the stone patio in the walled garden, with its lush greenery, palm trees, fish pond, and fountain. The inn is just a few blocks from the water, and the McMurrys provide bicycles for touring historic St. Augustine.

Accommodations: 5 rooms with private bath, and 2 suites. *Pets:* Not permitted. *Driving Instructions:* Take I-95 to the St. Augustine exit. Turn right and drive to King Street. Turn left and, at the historic slave market, turn right (through the Cochina Archway) onto Aviles Street.

THE KENWOOD INN

38 Marine Street, Saint Augustine, FL 32084. 904-824-2116. *Innkeepers:* Dick and Judi Smith. Open all year.

The Kenwood Inn, a fanciful, sprawling Victorian building in the heart of the historic district of the nation's oldest settlement, is half a block from Saint Augustine's waterfront and the Intracoastal Waterway. A real find anywhere but especially so in Florida.

Balconies, dormers, and gingerbread braces and supports jut out from every angle of the inn. One porch overlooks the new swimming pool. An inviting enclosed courtyard contains large pecan, plum, and grapefruit trees, as well as a fish pond and patio.

Each guest room has been decorated with coordinating wall paints, drapery, bedding, and thick terry towels. Each room is unique, one with lots of wicker, another with walnut pieces and marble-topped bureaus, another with scrolly Victorian oak. Three of the largest guest rooms have king-size beds and fireplaces. Several of the inn's bathrooms sport their original deep claw-footed bathtubs, for luxurious soaking.

Breakfast is a time enjoyed by guests and the innkeepers together, around the big dining-room table in the lobby area. A favorite topic discussed is other inns and innkeepers encountered on travels. In a

living room beyond the lobby, guests can relax and read; others prefer the inn's Florida room, home to the only television set in the house.

Accommodations: 16 rooms, most with private bath. *Pets and young children:* Not permitted. *Driving Instructions:* The inn is at the corner of Marine and Bridge streets in Saint Augustine's historic district.

WESTCOTT HOUSE

146 Avenida Menendez, St. Augustine, FL 32084. 904-824-4301. *Innkeeper:* Sheena E. Dennison. Open all year.

Dr. John Westcott moved to St. Augustine in 1858 and soon became associated with northern Florida's most celebrated citizen, Henry Flagler. Both Westcott and Flagler gained fame for their pioneering railroad efforts in the state. Dr. Westcott is also credited with the creation of that portion of the Intracoastal Waterway that runs from the St. John's River to Miami. In the 1880's, Westcott built a home overlooking the Matanzas River section of the Intracoastal Waterway. Today his home is painted pale coral with crisp white contrasting trim. Columned porches span the building's front two stories. Within, the guest and public rooms are among the most sumptuous offered in the city. The centerpiece of the parlor is an elaborate cast iron mantelpiece.

Each of the inn's eight guest bedrooms has been decorated in a different manner. Some have painted white iron bedsteads; others have the dark carved walnut beds characteristic of the high-Victorian period; while still others have stately brass beds. Complementing the period beds is an assortment of antique and reproduction furniture. All guest rooms have plus carpeting and private baths. Amenities at Westcott House are the rule, be it the complimentary wine offered or the sniffer of brandy left at one's bedside. Color television hidden in carved cabinets and room telephones are provided. Breakfast is delivered to guests' rooms on silver trays, or, if preferred, to the white iron tables and chairs set out in the brick courtyard behind the inn.

Accommodations: 8 rooms with private bath. *Pets and children:* Not permitted. *Driving Instructions:* Take U.S. 1 into St. Augustine and turn east on King Street. Drive to the bayfront and turn right on Avenida Menendez. Drive 2 blocks to the inn on the right.

Wakulla Springs, Florida

WAKULLA SPRINGS LODGE

1 Spring Drive, Wakulla Springs, FL 32305. 904-640-7011 or
904-222-7145. *Innkeeper:* John Puskar. Open all year.

Wakulla Springs has been attracting visitors for thousands of years,
during which the clear, deep-blue spring and its surroundings have
captured the interest and awe of most who have seen them. In the
early 1930s, Edward Ball, the financial genius of the Alfred Du Pont
estate, purchased thousands of acres of this wilderness cypress swamp
and spared no expense building the Wakulla Springs Lodge, a handsome Spanish-Moorish–style inn with marble and cypress used extensively throughout in the floors, stairways, tables, and bathrooms.

The beauty of the Wakulla Springs Lodge has never waned, just mellowed. The building has floor-to-ceiling Moorish arched windows across the entire front overlooking the springs and sanctuary. On the ground floor a spacious porch extends the length of the building. Comfortable wicker furniture and cool drinks await guests who relax here.

Behind the enclosed sun porch is the lobby-lounge. A large stone fireplace has plush chairs and couches grouped about it. The room is decorated with marble floors and has a beautiful ceiling, intricately painted by a German immigrant once commissioned by Kaiser Wilhelm. Every ceiling beam and cross-piece is covered with detailed pictures of the history of Wakulla Springs, its wildlife, Indians, and Spanish influences. Oriental rugs are scattered about groupings of Florida rattan furniture. Marble game tables complete the setting. A glass case in the lobby contains the remains of "Old Joe," the springs' legendary alligator, who was shot in the 1960s. "Old Joe," more than 11 feet long and weighing 650 pounds at his death, lived on a sandbar near the spring and in his day was the most photographed alligator in existence; his death made national news, and a $5,000 reward was offered for information leading to his killer.

Marble stairways and an elevator lead to the guest rooms. Some overlook the springs; others, the wild sanctuary; and still others, the profusion of flower gardens at the entrance to the springs. The furnishings are comfortable, quality pieces from the late 1940s and the 1950s, and each room has its own marble bath. Downstairs, the dining room, reminiscent of a European hotel with rocking-chair seating and white-linen service, offers Southern cooking at its best, including pan-fried chicken, mullets, and country ham accompanied by plates of fresh vegetables—black-eyed peas, baby limas, and navy beans. A favorite dish is the chef's special navy bean soup, on the menu every day by popular demand. There are Apalachicola oysters in season. There is no bar here, and liquor is not available.

Accommodations: 27 rooms with private bath. *Pets*: Not permitted. *Driving Instructions:* The Wakulla Springs Lodge is off Route 61, 11 miles south of Tallahassee.

PARK PLAZA HOTEL

307 Park Avenue South, Winter Park, FL 32789. 305-647-1072.
Innkeeper: Cissie Spang. Open all year.

Winter Park is a stylish town lined with boutiques and specialty shops and home to several museums, including the Morse Gallery, with its thousands of pieces of Louis Tiffany's work. In the center of town, alongside a shady park, is the Park Plaza. At street level there is little to attract attention to the hotel other than iron gates and flanking boutiques, one a fancy chocolate shop, the other for gifts and flowers. However, the second story veranda is quite eyecatching with its bower of hanging plants and potted flowers designed to screen guests from the street. The lobby has a distinct 1920s ambiance: Potted ferns and palms, polished dark woods, marble floors, and an open staircase lit by a roof-top skylight. The small private elevator glows with polished brass, and a big silver bowl of shiny red apples is set out on the reception desk. A sitting alcove has lace drapes on windows overlooking an enclosed courtyard of the restaurant next door.

The guest rooms upstairs are small, yet appealing, each with a brass bed, floral-print wallpaper, and its own sitting room furnished with antique wicker and calico prints, as well as paddle fans, television and telephones. Many of these rooms open onto the veranda.

Accommodations: 27 rooms with private bath. *Pets and children:* Not permitted. *Driving Instructions:* Take I-4 to the Fairbanks Avenue exit. Drive east to Park Avenue and turn left.

Georgia

Atlanta, Georgia

BEVERLY HILLS INN

 65 Sheridan Drive, N.E., Atlanta, GA 30305. 404-233-8520. *Innkeepers:* Bonnie and Lyle Kleinhans. Open all year.

In the quiet residential neighborhood of Buckhead stands the sedate little Beverly Hills Inn, built in 1929 in a symmetrical style chosen to resemble Hollywood architecture of the late 1920s. A parlor complete with a baby-grand piano and a well-stocked library occupy the inn's ground floor and are popular spots for guests to relax in or seek the innkeeper's assistance in planning the day's adventures or the best spot for an evening meal. Many restaurants within walking distance offer a variety of ethnic cuisines.

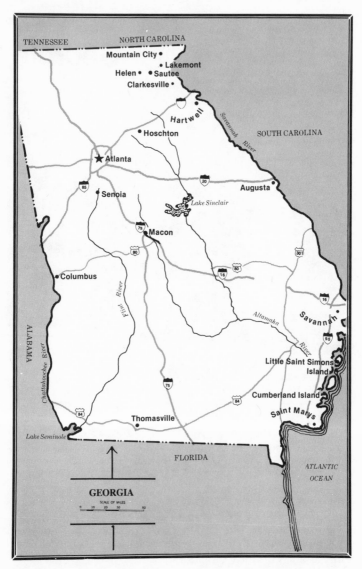

TENNESSEE

NORTH CAROLINA

Mountain City •
• Lakemont
Helen • • Sautee
Clarkesville •

Hartwell

SOUTH CAROLINA

Savannah River

• Hoschton

★ Atlanta

85

• Senoia

Augusta

20

75

• Macon

Lake Sinclair

80

16 80

301

• Columbus

Flint River

Altamaha River

Savannah

16

95

Chattahoochee River

Little Saint Simons Island

ALABAMA

75

84

Cumberland Island

Saint Marys

84

• Thomasville

Lake Seminole

FLORIDA

ATLANTIC OCEAN

GEORGIA

SCALE OF MILES

0   10   20   30   50

The inn is furnished throughout with many antiques and period pieces from the 1920s. Oriental rugs cover the natural hardwood floors. Most guest rooms open onto balconies through French doors; some of the rooms also have kitchens. An appealing Garden Room off the enclosed garden is the setting for Continental breakfasts.

Atlanta is a city of shopping areas, museums, music, theater, and other visitor attractions. The inn is convenient to much of this, its neighborhood featuring nearly thirty art galleries, as well as the large Lenox Square/Phipps Plaza with such stores as Neiman-Marcus and Tiffany's, just five minutes away.

Accommodations: 17 rooms with private bath. *Pets:* Not permitted. *Driving Instructions:* In Atlanta, take Peachtree Road north to Sheridan Drive.

Atlanta, Georgia

SHELLMONT BED AND BREAKFAST LODGE

821 Piedmont Avenue, N.E., Atlanta, GA 30308. 404-872-9290.

Innkeepers: Debbie and Edward McCord. Open all year.

Shellmont was built in 1891 by the architect W.T. Downing and is now listed in the National Register of Historic Places. When the McCords purchased the house in 1982, they were only its second owners. A distinctive feature is elaborate carvings both on the building's exterior and within. One dominant theme is shell carvings, augmented by ribbons and flowers. Stained, beveled, and leaded glass abound, and the reception area is adorned with elaborate stenciling. Both the main house and its carriage house are furnished in period antiques and have reproduction wall coverings with a different theme for each of the guest suites. Two in the Main House have fireplaces, and all three have access to a porch. The Carriage House, which accommodates one to four persons, has a living room with a double bed, a separate bedroom, and a fully stocked kitchen. Guests receive a basket of fruit, a split of wine, chocolates in the evening, the paper in the morning, and a complimentary Continental breakfast.

Accommodations: 3 rooms and cottage with private bath. *Pets:* Not permitted. *Children:* Permitted in the Carriage House only. *Driving Instructions:* From Route 29, drive north on Piedmont to the corner of Sixth Street.

Augusta, Georgia

TELFAIR INN

349 Telfair Street, Augusta, GA 30901. 404-724-3315. *Innkeeper:* Ms. Pat Hardy. Open all year.

Telfair Street and the Telfair Inn were named for Edward Telfair, Revolutionary War patriot and twice governor of Georgia. The street has a number of significant historic buildings and is part of a restored district called, today, Olde Towne. Olde Towne is within walking distance of the Savannah River and its waterfront area, where many early Augusta businesses prospered. A number of the most successful merchants in the city settled here and built their splendid Victorian homes nearby. The Telfair Inn is a product of the spirit of restoration that inspired the creation of the historic district that surrounds it.

The inn is actually a group of sixteen guest houses. Each is individually decorated and furnished to reflect the period of the buildings' construction, from 1860 to 1890. Some have working fireplaces, and many have whirlpool tubs in their bathrooms. Other modern conveniences include mini-refrigerators, wet bars, and cable television. The suites have kitchenettes. The inn also boasts an outdoor redwood hot-water spa, a swimming pool, and a Jacuzzi. The pool is terraced and landscaped and has a private patio where guests frequently elect to enjoy their complimentary Southern breakfast of eggs, sausage or bacon, biscuits, toast, grits, and coffee.

The Telfair Inn provides such personal services as placing fresh fruit in each guest room, serving afternoon cocktails at poolside, and offering complimentary limousine service to the local airport. Parking is available at the inn, and luncheon (as well as the complimentary breakfast) is served at the Fox's Lair, the inn's restaurant, which specializes in Greek dishes.

Accommodations: 96 rooms, 86 with private bath. *Driving Instructions:* The inn is in the heart of Augusta's "Olde Towne."

Clarkesville, Georgia

LaPRADE'S RESTAURANT, CABINS, AND MARINA

Route 1, Highway 197N, Clarkesville, GA 30523. 404-947-3312.
Innkeeper: Robert H. Nichols. Open April through November.

Mr. LaPrade built his camp in 1916 to house and feed engineers and workers who were harnessing the Tallulah River as a power supply. The result of their labors was Lake Burton, completed in 1925. Mr. LaPrade then had the good sense to turn his camp into a fishing retreat, which has evolved into a rustic Georgia mountain camp just off the Appalachian Trail. Its heart is the dining room, where people come from far and wide to enjoy the truly fresh, home-style Southern dinners. The owners operate three farms providing most of the meat and vegetables served — and the meals are noteworthy. Breakfast features country ham, sausage, red gravy, grits, eggs, hot biscuits, sorghum syrup, honey, and homemade jellies; lunch offers plenty of chicken and dumplings, one other meat, hot biscuits, corn bread, several vegetables, and a cobbler pie; dinners begin with onion relishes and coleslaw, run on through the specialty — fried chicken — or country ham with breads and vegetables, and end with a cobbler dessert. Drinks are included with the bountiful and inexpensive meals, which in turn are included in the room rates for guests.

Guests are reminded that this is essentially a fishing retreat. The food is good, but the cabins are very austere and rustic. Some can sleep up to twelve people each. The cabins are sprinkled around the property; two have fireplaces, and two others are at lakeside. Cabins have front porches with rockers and are outfitted with gas heat and indoor facilities. The camp's Game Room has pinball machines and ice and beverage machines. The marina offers rentals of fishing boats, canoes, pontoons, and motors. The lake and streams offer excellent fishing, boating, and swimming. The mountains provide fresh air and hiking woods. A gift shop sells mountain crafts.

Accommodations: 21 cabins with private bath. *Pets:* Not permitted. *Driving Instructions:* 18 miles north of Clarkesville on Route 197.

Columbus, Georgia

THE DE LOFFRE HOUSE

812 Broadway, Columbus, GA 31901. 404-324-1144. *Innkeepers:* Shirley and Paul Romo. Open all year.

The De Loffre House is an 1863 town house in the heart of the Columbus Historic District. On a brick-paved parkway, the Italianate house is the epitome of the Victorian period in Columbus.

Public rooms at the De Loffre House include a spacious entry hall that, with several sofas and a table and chairs, acts as an adjunct to the parlor. These rooms, and the second-floor sitting room, are furnished with Victorian and Empire antiques.

The De Loffre House has guest rooms where period lighting, tie-back curtains, and antique beds are the rule. Three of the rooms have a fireplace. Forgetful guests will be glad to find a shaver, shampoo, a shower cap, and books in the room. Upon arrival, guests will also find a decanter of sherry and a bowl of fresh fruit there. A complimentary Continental breakfast is served in the dining room on antique china by candlelight.

For those who wish to explore farther afield, the town of Plains, Georgia, is a short drive away, as are Franklin D. Roosevelt's "Little White House," Providence Canyon, 1850 Westville Village, and the beautiful Callaway Gardens.

Accommodations: 5 rooms with private bath. *Pets:* Not permitted. *Children:* Under twelve not permitted. *Driving Instructions:* The guest house is four blocks north of Route 280 and two blocks east of the river.

Cumberland Island, Georgia

GREYFIELD INN

Cumberland Island, Georgia. Mailing address: Drawer B, Fernandina Beach, FL 32034. 904-261-6408. *Innkeepers:* The Ferguson Family. Open all year.

Cumberland Island is the southernmost of the Georgia sea islands, saved from commercial development by being made part of the National Seashore. Access to the island is either by National Park Service boat from St. Mary's, Georgia, or by private boat from Fernandina Beach, Florida. The island is a fantasy land of live oaks, southern pines, and — by the sea — marsh grasses and rushes. The area abounds with wildlife including deer, raccoons, wild turkeys, alligators, squirrels, and wild pigs and horses. More than 150 species of birds have been spotted here and recorded by the National Park Service. Overnight accommodations on the island are provided by the Greyfield Inn. It is important to stress, however, that advance reservations are an absolute must and transportation arrangements must be confirmed.

The Greyfield Inn is the last remaining structure of the original Carnegie estate that once encompassed the entire island. The inn's current owners are descendants of Thomas Carnegie's. If you arrive by boat from Fernandina Beach, a Greyfield employee will meet you and drive you down the rough roads to the inn. There is something otherworldly about the drive along the narrow island road canopied by live oaks whose limbs have been shaped to form a tunnel almost blocking out the sun. Guests enter the inn through two rows of brick columns and walk up the broad staircase to the colonnaded front porch that spans the facade. Inside are faint memories of the Carnegie era. Many of the family antiques have been preserved, surrounded by the warmth of dark-stained wood paneling and painted or papered walls. Oriental rugs cover the floors, and turn-of-the-century lamps are the rule. The library's man-high shelves are filled with the classics. The downstairs rooms are softly lit, suggesting an English-style men's social club.

Upstairs are the guest rooms, ranging from some that are fairly small to the two-room "honeymoon suite," which has a sitting room and a bedroom containing a high-backed Victorian bed with an antique white spread.

After a simple breakfast, guests often explore the island on foot, taking along a picnic basket or returning to the inn for luncheon. At dinner, one entrée is prepared each day and dishes include roasts, seafood casseroles, or Southern-style ribs. The inn offers an opportunity for guests to retreat to an island wildlife refuge. The inn's services and accommodations cannot be described as sumptuous, and prospective guests must be warned that transportation on the island is primarily by foot. Those made nervous by wildlife should probably stay on the mainland. The days of luxurious meals served by an attentive staff of servants are far in the past, but the island is filled with eerie romance for those who seek it.

Accommodations: 10 rooms, sharing baths. *Pets:* Not permitted. *Driving Instructions:* Advance arrangements must be made for boat service and pickup by the inn.

WORLEY HOMESTEAD BED & BREAKFAST INN

410 W. Main Street, Dahlonega, GA 30533. 404-864-7002. *Innkeepers:* Mick and Mitzi Francis. Open all year.

Gold was discovered in the foothills of Georgia's Blue Ridge Mountains in 1828. By 1833 Dahlonega was a full-fledged gold rush town. (The name Dahlonega means precious yellow metal in the Cherokee language.) In 1838 a U.S. Mint was built on Worley land, across from what would one day be the Worley Homestead, an 1845 clapboard building with a classic second-story veranda shading a ground-floor entry. The inn was home to Captain William Worley, a distinguished town leader, who lived here until his death in 1913. The homestead later fell into disrepair and was in danger of being torn down when it was rescued by Captain Worley's great-granddaughter, Mitzi Francis, and her husband, Mick. They restored the house, transforming it into a bed-and-breakfast inn, its two porches lined with rocking chairs, complete with antique-filled guest rooms, parlor, and dining room, enhanced by a staff that dresses in costumes of the day.

Many rooms have working fireplaces — including a little romantic cottage on the grounds, which also has a canopied bed. Guests are greeted with trays of freshly baked cookies, candies, and fruit, while breakfasts include foods which would have been served in the late nineteenth century. The inn is set amid many historic buildings surrounding the old courthouse square, with its gold museum, shops, and country-style restaurants. Just outside of town are several places where one may still try panning for gold.

Accommodations: 9 rooms, 7 with private bath. *Pets:* Not permitted. *Driving Instructions:* From Atlanta take Route 400 to Dahlonega. The inn is two blocks west of the town square on Routes 52 and 9.

HARTWELL INN

504 West Howell Street, Hartwell, GA 30643. 404-376-3967. *Innkeeper:* Mary Jo Swanson. Open all year.

The Hartwell Inn in the rolling hills of northern Georgia is a well-preserved antebellum mansion surrounded by many pecan trees and formal gardens. In true Southern tradition there is a large veranda complete with porch swing and rocking chairs set behind towering white columns. It is one of Hartwell's oldest remaining estates of its kind. Guests enter through a large leaded-glass door into the foyer, which has highly polished hardwood floors and Oriental carpets. They are then given a get-acquainted tour of the public rooms before being shown upstairs to their own rooms. The drawing room, frequently with a fire in the hearth in the fall or winter, is a relaxing room, with reading material, games, and sherry set out for guests. The formal parlor has pre–Civil War furnishings and a grand piano for evening songfests. The high ceilings and leaded-glass windows add to the formal atmosphere. The guest rooms have a variety of antique pieces, including brass, iron, or wooden beds. All rooms have coal-burning fireplaces. Breakfast is served by candlelight in the dining room, which is set up with individual tables decorated in keeping with the season.

Accommodations: 5 rooms with shared bath. *Pets:* Not permitted. *Driving Instructions:* From I-85 take the Lavonia exit south. The inn is at the intersection of U.S. 29 and Route 77.

Helen, Georgia

THE HELENDORF INN

P.O. Box 305, Helen, GA 30545. 404-878-2271. *Innkeepers:* Dick and Barbara Gay. Open all year.

The Helendorf Inn, overlooking the Chattahoochee River, is a creation in Bavarian-style architecture. It combines the Old World look of balconies and a medieval tower with such modern conveniences as color television, telephones, individual heat and air-conditioning, and wall-to-wall carpeting. Walt Disney would understand the Helendorf's made-to-order make-believe and fun. Each of the guest rooms that overlook the river has a complete kitchen, a dining area, and a private balcony. If you want to go first class at the Helendorf, reserve the Bridal Suite perched atop the tower. It has a kitchenette, a sitting area, and a king-size bed.

The public rooms in the Helendorf are rustic, with fireplaces and heavy, exposed ceiling-beams. There is a large party-conference room with its own stone fireplace that is used for special events at the inn. No meals are served, but Helen has many German and American restaurants within easy walking distance.

Accommodations: 82 guest rooms with private bath. *Pets:* Permitted with additional charge. *Driving Instructions:* Take Route 17 or 75 to Helen. The inn is at the center of town, on the banks of the Chattahoochee.

Hoschton, Georgia

HILLCREST GROVE

Peachtree Road, Hoschton, GA 30548. 404-654-3425. *Innkeeper:* Dennis Pitters. Open all year.

This turn-of-the-century country house was once the centerpiece of the 2,000-acre Hill-family estate. Although the property now consists of 6 acres, the remainder of the original estate is preserved undeveloped behind the inn. Hillcrest Grove is sheltered by a grove of mature pecan trees in a woodland setting. The Neoclassical mansion took almost four years to complete, and the craftsmanship that went into the building is still evident. The prominent front porch is highlighted by Doric columns and two-story brick pillars, and mahogany is used throughout the interior.

Guests are ushered into a hall dominated by an open-well staircase. The library off this hall often has a fire in its hearth, making it a favorite gathering place for visitors in the cooler seasons. In summer the porch is inviting, with its lounge chairs and frequent refreshing breezes. The guest rooms are comfortably furnished, each has a fire-place, and bowls of fresh fruit are set out on the bureaus. Breakfast, the only meal served, features freshly baked pastries made with pecans from the inn's grove. Hillcrest Grove is an ideal starting point for a scenic drive through the north-Georgia mountains.

Accommodations: 3 rooms with shared bath. *Pets:* Not permitted. *Driving Instructions:* Hillcrest Grove is 44 miles northeast of Atlanta. Exit from I-85 at the Braselton-Hoschton interchange (number 49), then go south on Route 53 2½ miles to the entrance, by a pecan grove.

Lakemont, Georgia

Lakemont is part of Rabun County, famous for its setting used in the movie *Deliverance*. The Chattooga River offers excellent white-water conoeing and kayaking—as the movie illustrated so graphically. Wildwater Ltd. provides equipment and guides. Lake Rabun offers boating, canoeing, fishing, and swimming, with boat rentals and tackle shops. The lake is in the Chattahoochee National Forest wilderness, which has many fine hiking trails and mountain streams with waterfalls and excellent trout fishing. *Tallulah Falls Gorge,* the deepest in the eastern states, once had an enormous waterfall that is now reduced to a small stream. The gorge is off U.S. 441-23 near the Tallulah Falls campground. *Sky Valley Ski Slope* is located in nearby Dillard as is the popular Dillard House, famed for its Georgia food.

LAKE RABUN HOTEL

Lake Rabun Road, Lakemont, Georgia. Mailing address: Route 1, Box 101-A, Lakemont, GA 30552. 404-782-4946. *Innkeepers:* Dick and Barbara Gray. Open April 1 through October 30.

The Lake Rabun Hotel, an old, rustic inn, is across a narrow country road from one of Georgia's most beautiful lakes. In the heart of the Chattahoochee National Forest with its dogwoods, tall shade trees, wildflowers, ferns, and mosses, the hotel is constructed of dark woods and sturdy Georgia stones with planters and stone seats jutting from the stone foundations and chimneys. The inn, built in 1922, retains most of its original work and furnishings and all of its unique charm.

Here many lasting friendships are formed in the informal setting as guests gather around the rock fireplace that warms the lobby. The Lake Rabun Hotel could have come straight out of a fairy tale — couches, chairs, tables, even the picture frames are all handmade of twisty mountain laurel and rhododendron branches. The heart-pine and oak walls display original 1920s art, and the arches have been created out of old pine logs.

The guest rooms are decorated with ruffled tie-back curtains, simple country bedspreads, and colorful quilts that create the feel of a rustic cottage. Two of the rooms still have handmade beds, and most have sinks perked up with ruffled gingham skirts. Guest rooms are cooled by mountain breezes, and the tapwater comes straight from clear, cold mountain springs. No television or telephones jar guests out of this wilderness peace, but the smells of fresh home baking get one up and moving in the morning. Barbara and Dick offer a help-yourself Continental breakfast in the lounge by the fireside. This is the only meal served, but the neighborhood offers fine "down home" eating at such places as Dillard House and LaPrades Camp.

Accommodations: 16 rooms, 1 with private half bath and the others with shared baths. *Pets:* Not permitted. *Driving Instructions:* Lake Rabun is about 9 miles south of Clayton off U.S. 441-23. Drive 6 miles south of Clayton, then turn right at the Wiley Junction Store and the Clayton Carpet Cleaner. Turn sharp left and proceed 4 miles to the hotel on the right.

LITTLE SAINT SIMONS ISLAND

Mailing address: P.O. Box 1078CI, Saint Simons Island, GA 31522. 912-638-7472. *Innkeepers:* Ben and Laura Gibbens. Open February through October.

Every once in a while you are lucky enough to find an inn so private and in such a special setting that you almost feel you shouldn't write about it. One such place is Little Saint Simons Island. Reached only by boat, Little Saint Simons boasts an intriguing history. One of the fabled "Golden Isles" of Georgia, it is said to hide some of Blackbeard's buried treasure. Remnants of thousand-year-old Guale or Creek Indian villages dot the forest floor. Ruins of a tabby (stucco) dwelling built by early European settlers still exist among the thick foliage where wild horses and herds of German fallow deer hide.

The site of one of the first rice plantations on the North American continent, Little Saint Simons was home for a time to the famous English actress Fanny Kemble after her marriage to Pierce Butler. Her book condemning slavery touched off a furor during the years preceding the Civil War and led to her divorce from Butler. Just after the turn of the century, the estate was purchased by Philip Berolzheimer, an owner of the Eagle Pencil Company, which had harvested the largest of the island's red cedars. It has remained as a retreat for the Berolzheimer family ever since. Not long ago the island was opened to the general public on a very limited (twenty guests at a time) basis. Recent visitors have included President Jimmy Carter and Vice-President Walter Mondale.

Accommodations for overnight guests are in four buildings: the main lodge, a new cedar house, and two cottages. Each offers simple, rustic quarters filled with cedar paneling and such quaint country furniture as peeled-log bedsteads. On the walls of most rooms are mounted trophies of the rich hunting and fishing opportunities surrounding the estate. The food at Little Saint Simons reflects its country Southern heritage, offering fresh seafood (fish, crabs, shrimp, oysters, and clams) as well as other traditional dishes like country ham, chops, and fried chicken.

Little Saint Simons itself provides abundant activities for guests with its wealth of natural resources. The island employs two professional naturalists who are expert at steering guests in the right

direction for exploration. With 12,000 acres of private land, 8 miles of Atlantic Ocean beachfront, and virtually no development, finding a spot to explore is certainly no problem. Other activities include excellent bird watching, beachcombing, hiking, horseback riding, fishing, or just plain relaxing in seclusion. Along the beach, guests can explore for shore birds, sea turtles, and an abundance of shells. Oysters plucked from the water's edge can become a prelude to a memorable dinner. The possbilities are virtually endless. Stop a moment on one of the island's trails overhung by live oaks draped in Spanish moss and contemporary civilization seems to drift away.

Accommodations: 12 guest rooms, 8 with private bath. *Pets*: Not permitted. *Driving Instructions:* The island is reached only by boat. Guests are met at a private landing according to a schedule established when reservations are made. From Brunswick, Georgia, take the causeway to Saint Simons Island. Follow the signs to Sea Island until you get to the intersection of Frederica Road. Turn left (north) and go past Sea Palms Golf Course to Harrington Road, where a large red barn has been converted into a restaurant. Turn right and go to the dock at the end of the road.

Macon, Georgia

1842 INN

353 College Street, Macon, Georgia. Mailing address: P.O. Box 4746, Macon, GA 31208. 912-741-1842. *Innkeeper:* Aileen P. Hatcher. Open all year.

The 1842 Inn is fashioned from two buildings connected by a patio and garden. The main house is a classic antebellum Greek Revival mansion built in 1842, and the smaller is a later Victorian cottage. Together they provide twenty-two guest rooms, sitting rooms, and a formal room for small meetings, luncheons, or catered dinners. All are appointed with Oriental rugs, antiques, and period reproductions. Most of the guest rooms have working fireplaces, and some have

whirlpool baths and facilities for the handicapped, along with bouquets of fresh flowers and coordinated drapes, dust ruffles, and bed coverings. Modern conveniences include private baths, room telephones, color television, and central air-conditioning. A Continental breakfast is brought to each guest room along with the morning paper. Other amenities include turn-down service, a cocktail bar in the parlor, and overnight shoeshines. Although the Inn is located close to restaurants, historic sites, and Macon's business district, its landscaped grounds have been planted in keeping with the nineteenth-century atmosphere.

Accommodations: 22 rooms with private bath. *Pets:* Not permitted. *Driving Instructions:* From Macon, take I-16 to the Spring Street exit. Turn right and drive to Riverside Drive. Turn left on Riverside Drive and left again on College Street.

Mountain City, Georgia

THE YORK HOUSE

P.O. Box 126, Mountain City, GA 30562. 404-746-2068. *Innkeepers:* Ingrid and Philip Sarris. Open all year.

The York House is one of northern Georgia's oldest mountain inns. In 1896 "Uncle Bill" and "Little Mama" York opened the inn, beginning a long history of innkeeping for the family. The inn began as a two-story square-logged cabin on a thousand-acre plantation in the Little Tennessee Valley. The walls of the original cabin are now encased within the walls of the living room, den, and two of the guest rooms. The basement still contains a stone room where slaves were once quartered. A stone fireplace in the stone room marks the end of the log cabin, and the original hand-hewn beams and logs are still visible there.

At the turn of the century, nearby Tallulah Falls rivaled Niagara Falls and attracted many tourists to the region; the railroad increased business when it pushed on through Rabun County. However, when the Georgia Power Company diverted the river's waters to power its hydroelectric generators, Tallulah Falls disappeared. What remains is the oldest natural gorge in North America, more than 2,000 feet deep and a mile and a half long. Today the area is a railroad buff's delight, and many make pilgrimages here in search of remnants, including the old trestles in the nearby mountain passes.

The York House is a tranquil mountain retreat with two stories of shaded verandas overlooking its lawns, towering hemlocks and pines, and the mountains in the distance. The guest rooms, each with its own entrance, are located off these porches and breezeways. The inn's interior is simple and comfortable. Period furniture works to create an atmosphere of timelessness. The rooms have been restored and decorated, turn-of-the-century antiques combining with contemporary comforts such as the modern bathrooms and wall-to-wall carpeting. Full breakfasts served to guests in their rooms are the only meals offered, but there are many restaurants in the vicinity.

The Appalachian Trail can be entered a short distance away. White-water rafting and tubing are popular sports on the nearby Chatooga River, and Lakes Rabun and Burton offer swimming and camping as well as scenic waterfalls. Moviegoers may remember that the York House was featured in scenes at the very end of the movie *Deliverance*.

Accommodations: 14 rooms with private bath. *Pets:* Not permitted. *Driving Instructions:* York House is 5 miles north of Clayton on Route 23/441.

RIVERVIEW HOTEL

105 Osborne Street, St. Marys, GA 31558. 912-882-3242. *Innkeeper:* Jerry Brandon. Open all year.

The Riverview was built in 1916 alongside the Saint Marys River, which leads out to the Intercoastal Waterway and the Atlantic beyond. The hotel is a two-story stuccoed structure with columns supporting the top and bottom rows of verandas overlooking the river and downtown St. Marys. The hotel has been painstakingly renovated by the Brandons, who bought the Riverview and reopened it after a fifteen-year hiatus. The lobby and wide hallways are decorated to recapture the feeling of an early 1900s hotel. The completely renovated guest rooms have heavy, oaklike furnishings and private bathrooms with fiberglass tub showers. There is a comfortable sitting room on the second floor that opens onto the balconied porch lined with old rockers. The sitting room is outfitted with wicker couches and chairs with soft cushions, and the porch is a cool spot for relaxing and watching the shrimp boats and ferry. Breakfast is served at the Riverview every morning. Seagle's Restaurant and Lounge, on the first floor of the hotel, serves luncheon and dinner from a steak-and-seafood menu daily.

Across from the hotel is a small median that the Brandons had landscaped with palms and pink-blossomed oleanders. Ship's-ballast stones form the planters containing colorful flowers. Ferryboats that dock in the river across from the hotel carry passengers to and from the Cumberland Island National Seashore nearby.

Accommodations: 18 rooms with private bath. *Pets*: Not permitted. *Children:* No charge if under twelve. *Driving Instructions:* The inn is 11 miles east of Kingsland on Route 40. Take Route 40 to downtown St. Marys, where there is a dead end at the river. The hotel is on the right.

Sautee, Georgia

THE STOVALL HOUSE

Route 1, Sautee, Georgia. Mailing address: Box 103A, Sautee, GA 30571. 404-878-3355. *Innkeepers:* Ham and Kathy Schwartz. Open all year.

The earliest section of the Stovall House was built in 1837 by Moses Harshaw, reputed by his neighbors to be "the meanest man that ever lived." His meanness did not hinder his craftsmanship, and he constructed a fine house on a hillside overlooking cow pastures, a creek, and the distant mountains of northeastern Georgia. The following owner, a Mr. Stovall, ran the sawmill and made several additions. In 1983 Ham and Kathy Schwartz bought the house and began a careful restoration resulting in an appealing inn listed in the National Register of Historic Places. The wraparound vistas and cow pastures remain, along with twenty-eight of the property's acres.

Stovall House has high ceilings, original walnut woodwork, and a big veranda, complete with old-fashioned wicker and a porch swing. All the rooms are furnished with antiques set off by the polished wood floors and Kathy's decorative stenciling. Each bathroom has Victorian fixtures, including pull-chain toilets, pedestal sinks, and Victorian light fixtures. There are three dining rooms, where Ham and Kathy offer Georgia country food to guests and the public.

Accommodations: 5 rooms with private bath. *Pets:* Not permitted. *Driving Instructions:* Take Route 17 south from its junction with Route 75 (approximately 2 miles south of Helen) for 1½ miles to the junction of Route 255 (at Old Sautee Store); turn left and take Route 255 for 1½ miles to the Stovall House on the right.

Savannah, one of the South's most elegant and gracious historic cities, sits on a bluff above the Savannah River. General James Oglethorpe and a band of colonists made camp here and laid out America's first planned city in 1733. *Old Savannah* is now a registered national historic landmark, the largest urban area so designated in the country. It is a beautiful city of acre-square floral parks with monuments and fountains, historic homes in a great many architectural styles, ornamental ironwork and moss-covered Savannah-gray bricks, 200-year-old cemeteries, and Southern home cooking. Along the banks of the river is the restoration of Savannah's waterfront, *Riverfront Plaza*, and the charming cobblestone and iron-bridged *Factor Walk*.

There are so many things to see and do here it is almost impossible to list them, much less to give some background. Therefore, the best way to begin a visit to Savannah is to go to *Savannah's Visitors' Center* at 301 West Broad Street, at the end of Route I-16. The center is in the restored Georgia Central Railroad Station, built in 1860. It is open seven days a week from 8:30 to 5:00.

BALLASTONE INN

14 East Oglethorpe Avenue, Savannah, GA 31401. 912-236-1484.
Innkeeper: Tarby Bryant. Open all year.

The Ballastone Inn offers travelers Southern hospitality with a generous dash of European elegance. This is one of the most recent additions to the list of Savannah's fine, historic lodging places. Built in 1835, originally as a private residence, the inn is in the center of the historic district. This area was the first blueprinted in England and laid out by General James Edward Oglethorpe, founder of Savannah. His plans, with parks every few blocks, remain virtually unchanged today, and it is in this lovely parklike setting that one finds the Ballastone.

The inn's name has historic significance to the city. Ballastones were, quite literally, the stones used as ballast in the ships sailing from Europe. When the ships arrived, the ballast would be dumped and the ship's hold filled with bales of cotton for the trip back home. Many of these original ballastones can still be seen on River Street and on the ramps leading up from the riverfront.

The Ballastone is decorated with antiques gleaned from the area's many antique shops, as well as with carefully selected reproductions. The wall coverings and fabrics were designed by artist Ann Osteen and produced by Scalamandre, Inc., of New York as part of its Savannah Collection. The warm earthtones of the wall paints are from the Historic Savannah Foundation's "Savannah Colors" series. Included in four floors of fine Victorian pieces are elaborate armoires in place of closets, carved mirrors in each bath, romantic ceiling fans, and intimate sitting areas. The handsome beds in each room are reproductions of classic Savannah designs. Guest rooms have themes, with fabrics, rugs, wallcoverings, and, if possible, furniture related to such names as "The Gazebo," "China Trade," or "Hannah's Room."

At the garden level are smaller rooms, where casual wicker and Victorian oaken furnishings prevail, unlike the more formal upper-floor rooms with their English antiques. Modern amenities include room telephones, television, and elevator service.

In their totally renovated historic mansion, the innkeepers provide myriad special personal services characteristic of a first-class inn. Complimentary sherry is served, and there is brandy on the night table. Shoes left by the door are shined overnight. A Continental breakfast, Southern style, awaits guests each morning. In the afternoon, tea and cocktails are served under the shade of fragrant magnolias and wisteria in the beautifully landscaped courtyard.

Ballastone is a place in which the history and romance of the old South blends with the creature comforts of today.

Accommodations: 19 rooms with private bath. *Pets:* Permitted with additional charge. *Driving Instructions:* Take I-16 or I-95 into Savannah. The inn is on Oglethorpe Street, between Bull and Drayton streets.

THE BED AND BREAKFAST INN

117 Gordon Street West, Savannah, GA 31401. 912-233-9481. *Innkeeper:* Robert McAlister. Open all year.

The Bed and Breakfast Inn is a Federal townhouse built in 1853 as part of Gordon Row. This row, with its extraordinary ironwork, is considered to be among the finest of its period in the country. The townhouse, once the home of a wealthy cotton planter, overlooks Chatham Square, one of Savannah's beautiful parks, originally designed by the city's founder, General James Edward Oglethorpe. The inn is within an easy stroll of the riverfront and the district's museums, restaurants, and major historical sights.

Innkeeper Bob McAlister has carefully renovated the lovely old house, which previous owners had allowed to deteriorate until nothing was left but its shell. Today it is wonderfully restored, with polished wide-pine floors covered here and there with richly hued Oriental carpets. Freshly painted walls provide quiet backdrops for the antiques and period reproductions throughout the inn. Fresh flowers can be found in the parlor, original artwork decorates the walls, and

houseplants add touches of greenery to nooks and crannies.

There are two types of guest lodgings here—bed-and-breakfast rooms and garden apartments. The apartments are completely private suites opening onto a garden containing banana trees, flowering plants, and a fountain and fishpond. The suites have separate entrances, sitting rooms, color television, and kitchens. The bed-and-breakfast rooms, comfortable but simpler, have views of Chatham Square, as well as shared baths.

Accommodations: 6 rooms sharing 3 baths; 4 suites with private bath. *Pets:* Discouraged. *Driving Instructions:* The inn is on Gordon Street West between Barnard and Whitaker streets, across from Chatham Square.

ELIZA THOMPSON HOUSE

5 West Jones Street, Savannah, Georgia 31401. 912-236-3620. *Innkeeper:* Frank Gay. Open all year.

The Eliza Thompson House is a fine old townhouse built in 1847 for a beautiful redheaded widow and her seven children. "Miss Eliza" and other "ladies of property" used her enormous hearth to bake corn cakes for the Union soldiers in 1864. The corn cakes are now a tradition here and are baked daily and served as part of the inn's Continental breakfast.

Today, the townhouse is an attractive guest house where ceiling fans, courtyard fountains, handsome antique furnishings, fires in the inn's hearths, and the soft luster of the heart pine floors work to create a sense of Southern hospitality in a historic setting.

Accommodations: 17 rooms with private bath. *Pets:* Not permitted. *Driving Instructions:* The inn is in the historic district, off Bull Street, between Madison and Monterey squares, two parklike areas.

FOLEY HOUSE INN

14-16 West Hull Street, Savannah, GA 31401. 912-232-6622; toll free: 800-647-3708 (out of state). *Innkeeper:* Suzanne S. Davis. Open all year.

Foley House Inn overlooks Chippewa Square, with its palms and Spanish moss. The brick-faced inn is composed of two town houses, one built in 1896 and the other in 1870, joined by a stairwell.

The inn is appointed with many antiques, Oriental rugs, pencil-post four-poster beds, and porcelains. Fifteen of the twenty guest rooms have fireplaces, many with elaborately carved mantles. Several guest bathrooms have oversize Jacuzzis, and most are equipped with remote-control television with video-disc players. Breakfast is served on a silver tray with delicate bone china and sterling silver. There are cheesecakes, buttered croissants, and fresh fruits. Guests can take their breakfast, the only meal served at the inn, in their room or out in the sunny courtyard. Guests are offered complimentary cocktails on arrival, turn-down service with chocolates on the pillow, shoe shines, and use of the outdoor Jacuzzi, which accommodates up to eight people. A private limousine will meet arriving guests at the airport if they wish.

Accommodations: 20 rooms with private bath. *Pets:* Not permitted. *Driving Instructions:* From Florida or South Carolina take I-95. From Atlanta take Route 75 south to I-16 east. The inn is on Hull Street between Bull and Whitaker streets.

GREYSTONE INN OF SAVANNAH

24 East Jones Street, Savannah, GA 31401. 912-236-2442. *Innkeepers:* Woody and Jeanne Cunningham. Open all year.

Greystone Inn is an 1858 brick townhouse offering guests the best of two worlds: Period furnishings amid the elegance of gracious old Savannah together with the comforts of modern private bathrooms, color television, and air-conditioning. The carefully restored house is decorated with bold floral-patterned wallpapers, echoed by the rich color-coordinated trim. One guest room is painted in deep blues and reddish oranges, with a rich red-orange trim, while another highlights the khaki tans of the background colors of its Oriental carpet and wallpaper with dark-blue floral designs. The rooms are furnished with many eighteenth- and early-nineteenth–century pieces purchased in Charlestown. The parlor–sitting room has French and English wallpapers and period antiques. Two guest suites have kitchens. Breakfast is a full Southern affair, with curried fruits, quiches, grits, and the like. There is a quiet little garden and coveted off-street parking.

Accommodations: 7 rooms with private bath. *Driving Instructions:* The Inn is on East Jones Street, between Bull and Drayton streets.

LIBERTY INN

128 West Liberty Street, Savannah, GA 31401. 912-233-1007. *Innkeepers:* Frank and Janie Harris. Open all year.

When Colonel William Thorne Williams, six-term mayor of Savannah, decided to have a dwelling built for himself in 1834, he chose sturdy materials: local brick overlaid with clapboard. The construction allowed the building to survive several devastating fires that marked Savannah's early years. After the Civil War, the home became known as the "Dent House," and Miriam Dent, wife of a Savannah tinsmith, lived there until her death in 1931.

The stately, historic townhouse was saved from destruction by

Frank and Janie Harris, who bought it in 1967. They have a sentimental attachment to the building. On their very first date, in 1949, they went to the Liberty Café, which occupied its ground floor. Eighteen years and five children later, they purchased the neglected property and in 1979, following a thirteen-month restoration, opened their home to guests.

Today, the Liberty Inn offers accommodations in four suites, two with two rooms and two with three rooms. Each suite has a private entrance, air conditioning, a telephone, and cable television. The carpeted rooms have handsome appointments such as the original fireplaces, exposed interior brick walls, and original ceiling beams. Brass beds and period pieces blend with more modern furnishings. Shuttered windows open onto Liberty Street or onto the enclosed garden at the rear of the building, which contains the inn's 8-foot whirlpool spa and a grape arbor.

On the first floor, guests are welcome to enjoy the Liberty-Dent parlor, with its cypress fireplaces, elaborate arched doorways, and authentic Savannah colors. Each suite has a fully equipped kitchenette whose larder is supplied with Continental breakfast provisions, so guests can enjoy breakfast at their own pace each morning.

Accommodations: 4 suites with private bath for each bedroom. *Pets:* Not permitted. *Driving Instructions:* The inn is on Liberty Street, two blocks east of the I-16 exit.

MAGNOLIA PLACE

503 Whitaker Street, Savannah, GA 31401. 912-236-7674. *Innkeeper:* Howard I. Price, II. Open all year.

Magnolia Place is one of the grandest of Savannah's guest houses, a magnificent 1878 Victorian overlooking Forsyth Park. Its courtyard and grounds are landscapped with plants commonly used in Victorian times — banana, palms, tea olives and other exotica. A reflecting pool in the garden is home to Japanese carp and coy, while a decidedly unVictorian screened hot tub is tucked into a corner. The house itself is wonderfully High Victorian, with elaborate parquet, marquetry, crown moldings, tiled fireplace surrounds, and delicate woodwork. An open grand staircase is lit by an occulus thirty feet above the parlor floor. The rooms are furnished and decorated with collections of English Georgian antiques, Oriental carpets, porcelains, and brass and silver accessories purchased around the globe. The drapes, upholstery, and bedspreads are all appropriate to the Victorian period. The pencil-post canopied beds are reproductions in king and queen sizes. There are ten working fireplaces throughout the inn, along with several whirlpool baths, color television, and video cassette recorders, complete with a well-stocked library of cassettes.

The parlor has a wonderful melange of antique prints, porcelains, and assorted collections of butterflies, strikers, and brasses. Breakfast at Magnolia Place is served in the bedrooms, in the parlor, on the porch, or in the courtyard, supplemented by complimentary wine at check-in and hand-rolled chocolate truffles and brandy at bedtime. A classic Bentley town car is available to pick up guests at the airport or to take them to dinner.

Accommodations: 13 rooms with private bath. *Pets:* Not permitted. *Driving Instructions:* In Savannah take I-16 to the end and turn right on Liberty Street at the light. Drive to Whitaker Street and turn right. Go past the next traffic light (Gaston Street). The inn is the second house on the right.

17 HUNDRED 90

307 East President Street, Savannah, GA 31401. 912-236-7122.
Innkeeper: S. Izaddoost. Open all year.

The 17 Hundred 90 Inn is in the heart of Savannah's historic district. The beautiful old home is a Savannah Federal; its ground floor is of Savannah-gray bricks, the upper two stories of white clapboarding with shuttered "nine-over-nine" windows. For several years the inn has been a successful restaurant commanding rave reviews. *Gourmet* magazine called it "Savannah's most elegant restaurant." It seemed a natural second step to open the upper floors to guests wishing to savor Savannah's gracious Southern life. The inn is restored and furnished throughout with eighteenth-century antiques, Oriental rugs, and period reproductions of the drapery, wall coverings, and fabrics of Savannah's historic homes.

The inn is actually made up of two Federal-style houses joined together. The restaurant on the ground floor has the original gray flagstone floors, brick walls, arches, and fireplaces (there are a total of twenty-six working fireplaces in 17 Hundred 90).

Each of the rooms upstairs is individually decorated for guests; some are starkly modern but most have antiques, wallpapers, fabrics, and furnishings similar to those found in historic Savannah homes. Each room has an outer wall of exposed gray brick and a working gas-burning fireplace enclosed by glass doors for safety. The fires can be turned on and off by a bedside switch. One room has a large skylight over the bed alcove that is covered with a mirror at the push of a switch. The rooms are softly lit by crystal chandeliers, and Oriental rugs are soft for the feet. Private tiled bathrooms come equipped with adjustable shower-massages. The management spoils and pampers guests with bottles of complimentary wines at bedside; breakfasts of coffee, juice, and fresh buttery pastries brought to the rooms in the morning; and hideaway color television sets providing cable reception and free "cable movies." Guests are treated to limousine service to and from the airport when the car is available. For guests' relaxation there is a little sitting room upstairs and the inviting ground-floor lounge.

The 17 Hundred 90 restaurant offers guests and the general public haute cuisine in an eighteenth-century atmosphere. The shuttered room is sparked by tropical plants in the glass-covered atrium. Specialties here are fresh seafood in a variety of sauces, rack of lamb, chateaubriand, shrimp flambéed in sherry, and veal dishes. Caesar salads are assembled at the tables, and garden-fresh vegetables and "warm from the oven" breads accompany the main courses. There is a good selection of wines as well.

Accommodations: 14 rooms with private bath. *Pets and Children:* Not permitted. *Driving Instructions:* The inn is at the corner of Lincoln and President Streets in the heart of the historic district, one block from the Davenport and Owens-Thomas historic houses.

Senoia, Georgia

THE CULPEPPER HOUSE

Morgan at Broad Street, Senoia, Georgia. Mailing address: P.O. Box 462, Senoia, GA 30276. 404-599-8182. *Innkeeper:* Mary A. Brown. Open all year.

Senoia is a small, old-fashioned Southern town just south of Atlanta. This is *Gone with the Wind* territory, ideal for historical sightseeing and antiquing. The Culpepper House was built in 1871 by a returning Confederate veteran, Dr. John Addy. It served for five generations as the home of one of the area's physicians, Dr. Culpepper. The house's newest owner, Mary Brown felt it would be just right for a bed-and-breakfast inn and set about restoring it in 1982. Interested in historic preservation, she caters to guests who share her love of old houses.

The Culpepper House is an example of Queen Anne architectural style, both inside and out. The gingerbread trim on the wraparound porch is matched by the trim on the staircase inside. There are curved walls, Victorian oaken fretwork in doorways, stained glass, and pocket doors. Ms. Brown filled the rooms with Victorian antiques, Oriental carpets, and European and Oriental collectibles. She serves guests Continental breakfast in the old-fashioned kitchen, which has a stone hearth. Senoia and its neighboring towns have interesting restaurants and tearooms, and Ms. Brown will help guests plan outings, including meals and tours.

Accommodations: 3 rooms, 1 with private bath. *Pets:* Not permitted. *Driving Instructions:* Take Route 85 from Atlanta through Fayetteville to Route 16. Turn right and drive to Broad Street. Turn right again and drive to the corner of Morgan Street.

Thomasville, Georgia

SUSINA PLANTATION INN

Meridian Road, Thomasville, Georgia. Mailing address: Route 3, Box 1010, Thomasville, GA 31792. 912-377-9644. *Innkeepers:* Anne-Marie and Robert Walker. Open all year.

If you have ever wondered what it would be like living the antebellum life of a Scarlett O'Hara, here is your chance to find out firsthand. Susina Plantation, which opened its doors to the public as an inn in 1980, comes with imposing ionic columns on a classic Southern plantation-house facade. Its Spanish-moss–bedecked oaks, grand halls, spiral staircase, and magnificent chandeliers combine to create "one of the finest plantation houses in the region," according to the description in the National Register of Historic Places—and this is a region that abounds in plantations. The classic square Greek Revival mansion was built in 1841 for James Joseph Blackshear, a wealthy plantation owner with 8,000 acres and 102 slaves.

Inside the house, the work of noted nineteenth-century architect John Wind, one finds a spacious lounge and a dining room with tall windows overlooking the grounds. The rooms have wainscoting, paneled doors, and fireplaces offering welcoming fires on cool evenings. Meals at Susina Plantation are friendly affairs where guests dine together around an antique hand-carved mahogany table under a crystal chandelier. Included in the room rate are a breakfast and dinner with wine, fresh seasonal vegetables and fruits, freshly prepared soup, and a special entrée such as fish au gratin or roast beef. The cakes, pastries, and breads are baked daily in the inn's kitchen. Upon their arrival, guests are offered a glass of homemade wine.

The inn's guest rooms are furnished with antiques, Oriental rugs, and many Empire-style mahogany pieces. Some of the rooms have antique four-poster beds and hand-crocheted bedcovers. There are large claw-footed tubs in many of the bathrooms.

It is a pleasure to stroll the landscaped grounds with their sweeping lawns, tall shade trees dripping moss, and islands of flowering shrubs and sweet-scented dogwood and magnolias. In all, the inn is surrounded by 115 acres of meadows and woodlands. There is a 3-acre stocked pond as well as a floodlit tennis court and a new 50-foot-long swimming pool. For the incorrigibly lazy, the graceful sweep of verandas awaits, with couches, rockers, and porch swings.

Accommodations: 8 rooms, 7 with private bath. *Pets:* Permitted outside. *Driving Instructions:* Take the Meridian Road (Route 155) from Tallahassee 22 miles north to the inn, or follow signs off Route 319.

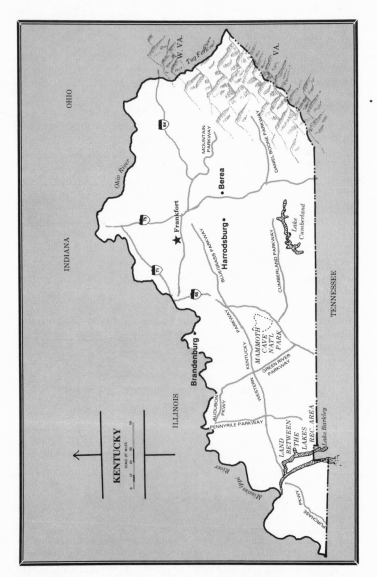

Kentucky

BOONE TAVERN HOTEL

Main Street, Berea, KY 40403. 606-986-9358/9359. *Innkeeper:* Miriam Pride. Open all year.

Boone Tavern is a handsome, white-brick Georgian-style hotel built in 1909 with the aid of student workers. It is operated by a staff composed mostly of students participating in the mandatory student work program at Berea college. Many of the students are hotel-management majors, so that the work experience they gain can be applied in their careers as well as providing financial support. The work program is immediately evident as one enters the inn. Almost all of the furniture in the lobbies and the dining rooms was made by the woodcraft program at the college. Pictures of Abraham Lincoln and Daniel Boone hang on the lobby walls, and the Lincoln lobby has a fireplace, although it has not been used in recent years.

There are two dining rooms at the tavern. The main dining room seats about two hundred, and there is a somewhat smaller private dining room. The menu at the tavern represents the heights to which Southern "home cooking" can aspire. The kitchen staff has gone out of its way to train prospective chefs and food-service experts, and the results are apparent in the food quality and the cheerful table service. Dinner selections change daily, but a representative sampling might include roast beef, chicken flakes Elsinore with sweet-pepper jam and buttered rice, roast turkey with Southern dressing, broiled Chinook salmon with lemon butter, roast leg of veal oregano, and our candidate for the dish with the best name: pork chops—some tricky way. All dinners start with one of the tavern's special soups (such as broccoli Roquefort, tomato bouillon, or pureed vegetable) and have

relishes, rolls, and Southern spoonbread. Also included are a salad of the day and a choice of two vegetables from a list of six. Desserts also vary each day with such possibilities as gooseberry pie with hard sauce, Jefferson Davis pie, nut tortes, French coconut pie, or Prince of Wales cake. Fresh flowers decorate the tables.

All guest rooms, which are on the top two floors, have beds, dressers, and chairs made in the woodcraft program, and the woven coverlets are from the student weaving programs.

Accommodations: 57 rooms with private bath. *Driving Instructions:* Take the Berea exit off I-75. The hotel is in the center of the Berea College campus, on Main Street.

DOE RUN INN

Brandenburg, KY 40108. 502-422-2982/2042. *Innkeeper:* Michael
Brown. Open all year exept Christmas Eve and Christmas.

Doe Run Inn is one of those special discoveries inn-lovers make and
are reluctant to share with anyone else. The wooded setting is en-
chanting and Daniel Boone's brother, Squire Boone, thought so too.
In 1778, Squire and a friend, John McKiney, discovered the stream
that runs past the inn. It is a branch of the Ohio River, and they
named it Doe Run for the many deer they saw. The oldest part of the
inn was begun in 1792, before Kentucky became a state, and the newer
part was finished about 1821. It is constructed of heavy, hand-hewn
timbers and thick native limestone block. The walls are more than 2
feet thick, and the front door was meant to withstand Indian attacks.
Abraham Lincoln's father worked as a stonemason on the building,
which began as a woolen mill and has seen service as a gristmill.

The mill and now the inn have been in Michael Brown's family for
six generations. Many family heirlooms and old milling equipment
are in use today at Doe Run. The two millstones are embedded in the
front walk, the enormous round wooden millstone cover is used as a
bench in the lobby, flour sifters are end tables, and the old oak office
standing desk still serves. The mill's flour-barrel copper stencils flank
the original stone fireplace downstairs. The inn is a stately stone
building with a big screened-in porch overlooking the swiftly running
stream and the woods. In warm weather, the porch is a favorite spot.

The inn's interior is rustic, with thick beams supporting the
ceilings. The limestone walls are exposed and in some places white-
washed. Floors are bare wood in the lobby, and the furnishings are a
blend of antiques and family heirlooms. Several of the old kerosine
lamps have been converted to electricity. Guests enjoy exploring the
inn and discovering the antiques and old prints and advertising art. A
tall secretary graces the lobby, and a 100-year-old organ still pumps
out tunes. There are old spinning wheels, butter churns, and even
yokes used by the oxen carrying flour from the mill.

Of the twelve guest rooms upstairs, those on the third floor are
austere but comfortable, resembling nineteenth-century accommodations. The second-floor rooms have more elegant furnishings; the

honeymoon suite is decorated with a marble-topped dresser, ornate mirror, and carved walnut bed, all from the Brown family. The hallway is a treasure trove of antiques, including a solid cherry chest carried down the Ohio River to the inn well before the Civil War, and a 150-year-old walnut chair with hand-woven tapestry covering that belonged to Wash Coleman, Michael's great-great-grandfather.

The inn serves three meals a day, every day. The dining room, open to guests and the public, offers Kentucky "down home" cooking. Favorites are the Kentucky country ham with red-eye gravy and the "honest to goodness" Kentucky fried chicken with cream gravy. All meals come with hot homemade biscuits, salads, vegetables, juice, and coffee or tea. The favorite dessert is the inn's special lemon pie. Lunches offer the ham and chicken, and a hearty breakfast might consist of juice, country ham with red-eye gravy, two eggs, baked apples, hot biscuits with butter and jelly, and hot coffee or tea. Smorgasbords, with a groaning board of more than eighty kinds of hot and cold dishes, are served Fridays from 5:30 to 9:00 and Sundays from noon to 9:00. Fridays feature seafood, and Sundays, fried chicken.

Accommodations: 13 rooms, 5 with private bath. *Driving Instructions:* The inn is 4 miles southeast of Brandenburg, Kentucky, on Route 448.

Harrodsburg is the oldest permanent English settlement west of the Allegheny Mountains. It was established June 16, 1774, by Colonel James Harrod, who directed the erection of Fort Harrod by Daniel Boone, Benjamin Logan, and John Floyd. At the original fort, George Rogers Clark planned his successful Revolutionary War campaign. The fort has been reconstructed and is now part of *Old Fort Harrod State Park*. On the park grounds are the reconstructed log stockades; the *Mansion Museum*, a brick mansion built in 1830; an early *school building*; *pioneer cabins*; and the *Lincoln Marriage Temple*. All the buildings contain artifacts from pioneer days. The cemetery is the oldest west of the Alleghenies. Every summer from mid-June through August there is a nightly (except Sunday) production of *The Legend of Daniel Boone* in the park amphitheater. The play, by Jan Hartman, chronicles the life of Boone and his contemporaries, including George Rogers Clark, Davy Crockett, Meriwether Lewis, Kit Carson, and Jim Bridger. For ticket information, write P.O. Box 365, Harrodsburg, KY 40330, or call 606-734-3346.

BEAUMONT INN

638 Beaumont Drive, Harrodsburg, KY 40330. 606-734-3381. *Innkeepers:* Mr. and Mrs. T. C. Dedman, Jr., and Mr. and Mrs. C. M. Dedman. Open mid-March to mid-December.

The Beaumont Inn is a fine old Kentucky establishment on one of Harrodsburg's seven gently rolling hills in the heart of the historic blue-grass region. It is a large brick building with a row of tall white columns aross its façade, surrounded by thirty well-groomed acres of partially wooded grounds with rolling lawns and hedges. Here visitors can find almost every kind of native tree and bush Kentucky has to offer; there are persimmons, maples of all shapes and sizes, ash, white pine, and, of course, magnolias.

The Beaumont was built in 1845 as the Greenville Institute, a school for young ladies. In 1855, it became Daughters' College, and after 1894 was known as Beaumont College, until it was purchased by Mrs. Goddard, the grandmother and great-grandmother of the present innkeepers, Bud Dedman and his son Chuck. Mrs. Goddard, who graduated from Daughters' College in 1880 and returned to

teach, eventually became Dean of Beaumont. Her daughter, who attended the school and later took over innkeeping from Mrs. Goddard, has been followed by her son and now her grandson. The Beaumont Inn has received acclaim from newspapers, magazines, and national travel guides. It was recently added to the National Register of Historic Places. The inn and its four generations of friendly inn-keepers deserve the warm praise; the place is a well-run, beautifully appointed hostelry, with good Kentucky home cooking.

The inn has been expanded to include two somewhat newer buildings housing additional guest rooms furnished with family antiques and comfortable stuffed chairs for lounging. Some even have the old fireplaces. Tree-shaded grounds can be seen through the white-curtained windows. Two guest suites are in a restored 1921 cottage decorated in early American.

The Beaumont offers fine tennis on newly surfaced (Chevron) courts, swimming in the large pool, which has lights for night use, and many lawn games, such as shuffleboard. The main house contains dining rooms, parlors, meeting rooms, and lounges. The parlors, reminders of the refined old college, have carpeting, rows of crystal tear-drop chandeliers, gilded mirrors above the old mantels, and comfortable wing chairs. During Derby week, parties and private cocktail fêtes are held here.

Hungry diners flock from all over for the Beaumont's famous two-year-old Kentucky-cured country ham or fried chicken, which are offered as the house specialty in tandem. The meal comes with fluffy corn pudding, far mcre like a soufflé than a pudding, and a wide choice of salads, including tomato aspic, cranberry-orange salad, and fruit salad. The favorite finale is General Robert E. Lee's orange-lemon cake, a house specialty. Several times a week the menu features a dish invented by Bud and his mother called mock scalloped oysters. The secret recipe is never revealed, and Mr. Dedman assured us that no one has ever guessed the ingredients—and it really does taste like scalloped oysters!

Accommodations: 29 rooms with private bath. *Pets:* Not permitted. *Driving Instructions:* From Harrodsburg, go south on U.S.127. The entrance is on the east side of the highway, ¾ mile from downtown.

SHAKERTOWN AT PLEASANT HILL

3500 Lexington Road, Harrodsburg, KY 40330. 606-734-5411. *Innkeeper:* Ann Voris. Open daily all year except Christmas Eve and Christmas Day.

To understand the Shakers is to understand the beauty-in-simplicity of this restoration, where all accommodations are in the original buildings, furnished as they would have been one hundred and fifty years ago. The Shakers were organized in the late eighteenth century. Part of their religious life involved frenetic shaking and whirling dances, which earned them the derisive title "Shaking Quakers," later shortened to "Shakers," a term they came to use themselves.

The Pleasant Hill village began in 1805, and by 1820 the colony had grown to nearly 500 inhabitants and was prosperous and self-sustaining. The buildings of the village were strikingly handsome, constructed generally of brick or stone under the architectural direction of Micajah Burnett. The graceful twin curving stairways in the Trustees' House are considered his finest artistic achievement.

Today, twenty-seven buildings survive and have been restored at Shakertown. The village now looks much as it did from 1820 to 1850, with a narrow dirt road running the length. The buildings represent the remains of five separate communal living groups called "families."

Visitors to the village may leave their cars in the parking lot and explore the restored village on foot. Although the original road through the village is restricted to pedestrian traffic, a service road runs around the village perimeter, and there is parking behind each of the fourteen restored buildings that have rooms for accommodations. Each guest room has been furnished with authentic reproductions of Shaker furniture. Bedspreads are hand-woven by Kentucky craftsmen, as are curtains and rugs. Some of the rooms are furnished with trundle beds. Each piece of furniture is a copy of an original found in the Center Family House museum. Rooms have concealed air conditioning and all have private baths. In place of closets, rooms have Shaker pegs on all walls.

The Trustees' Office, a three-story brick building built in 1839, is the most elaborate of the structures at Pleasant Hill. There are four dining rooms in the building and several overnight rooms on the two floors above.

Throughout the village, the staff is costumed, as are the waitresses in the dining rooms, which specialize in authentic Kentucky cooking.

Dinner offerings include fried chicken, country ham, fresh fish and steaks, and a daily special. Breakfast and lunch are also served. The management of the dining rooms prohibits tipping (as does the entire village).

The Shaker village is open all year, but crafts demonstrations are suspended from December 1 through mid-March. Two craft shops sell Kentucky handicrafts; and nearby, at Shaker Landing Road, a paddle-wheel riverboat offers cruises from May through October.

Accommodations: 72 rooms with private bath. *Driving Instructions:* The inn is on Route 68, 7 miles east of Harrodsburg.

Louisiana

Natchitoches, Louisiana

FLEUR DE LIS INN

336 Second Street, Natchitoches, LA 71457. 318-352-6621. *Innkeepers:* Bert and Mary Ann Froeba. Open all year.

Dating from 1714, Natchitoches, the oldest community in the Louisiana Purchase, has taken pride in preserving its many historic homes and cobblestone streets and has re-created Fort St. Jean Baptiste as it existed in 1732. Natchitoches is also the home of Northwestern University, and many college-related activities are available all year. Fleur de Lis, a many-gabled, turn-of-the-century Victorian house with rockers on its porch, is in the town's Historic District and within walking distance of the riverbank. Its large foyer, living room with a color-television, and dining room are all available to guests. Breakfast, served in the latter room at a 12-foot-long cypress table, includes homemade biscuits, eggs, grits, sausage, fruit, juice, and coffee. The inn's five large guest rooms are furnished in the style of the late Victorian period, with brass, Shaker, and testered beds from several periods. Some rooms have sitting areas, and all rooms display the Froebas' collection of period decorative pieces and memorabilia. Fresh fruit and sherry are put out for guests.

Accommodations: 5 rooms with private bath. *Pets:* Not permitted. *Driving Instructions:* From Alexandria, take Route 1 north to Natchitoches. Follow Route 1 across the bridge and turn left on Second Street.

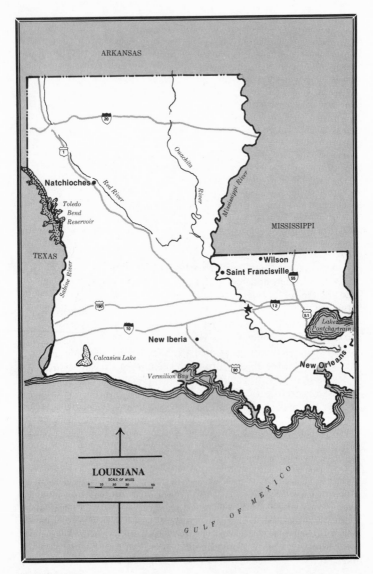

New Iberia, Louisiana

MINTMERE PLANTATION HOUSE

1400 East Main Street, New Iberia, LA 70560. 318-364-6210. *Inn-keeper:* Virginia Jones. Open all year except major holidays.

Mintmere Plantation House stands on 3 oak-shaded acres of lawn stretching down to the historic Bayou Teche, in the heart of "Cajun Country," or Acadiana. The house faces the tranquil bayou, once the main mode of transportation here. Mintmere was built in 1857 as a comparatively small plantation with only eight rooms. It is a Greek Revival Louisiana raised cottage, of a style fairly common in the South from the eighteenth century through the Civil War.

Today the house and grounds have been restored by Dr. Roy P. Boucvalt to form an oasis in an area that has seen extensive development. It is furnished throughout with Louisiana antiques of the American Empire, early-Louisiana, and Victorian periods. One guest room has heavy Empire furniture from New Orleans and paddle fans, while another has a cherry armoire and a large tester bed. Guests have the use of the parlor and flower-bedecked gallery overlooking the bayou and a duck pond. A light breakfast is served in the plantation's formal dining room.

Mintmere shares grounds with the restored Broussard House, an Acadian plantation house built in 1790 which houses two more suites. Both are open for public tours, as is Shadows-on-the-Teche a mile away.

Accommodations: 5 rooms, 4 with private bath. *Pets:* Not permitted. *Children:* Under twelve not permitted. *Driving Instructions:* Take Route 14 to New Iberia. At St. Peter Street turn right; then continue for 1¼ miles to Caroline Street and turn left. Drive one more block to the inn.

FRENCH QUARTER MAISONNETTES

1130 Chartres Street, New Orleans, LA 70116. 504-524-9918.
Innkeeper: Mrs. Junius W. Underwood. Open August 1 through
June 30.

The French Quarter Maisonnettes are seven modern guest rooms,
each with a private entrance off the brick and flagstone courtyard of
an old New Orleans home. The rooms are part of the 1825 townhouse
built by attorney Robert Soniat du Fossat, of the wealthy aristocratic
family whose prosperous plantation once occupied the land that is
now uptown New Orleans. The pale mauve stuccoed home has the
classic symmetry of the Creole houses, with a wrought-iron balcony
across the second story supported by graceful S-shaped braces. The
ground floor has a center iron gateway leading to a wide, arched carriage drive and the flagstone courtyard beyond. Black-shuttered, full-
length windows and French doors flank the carriageway and,
upstairs, the wide doorway onto the balcony. For more than one
hundred and fifty years, two iron horseheads have guarded the gate
and will probably do so for another century or two. Inside the iron
gates of the house are several wide French doors with arched transoms
opening onto the patio and drive. The interior gate mirrors the arch
with fanlike spokes in its iron top. The patio is filled with cherry
laurels, a large oak, and tropical plants and vines. Comfortable
lounge chairs are placed about for guests' convenience. The courtyard's centerpiece is a three-tiered fountain cast in France in the seventeenth century, its base filled with water lilies. In one corner of the
courtyard, a tiny iron spiral staircase leads from the balconies to the
ground. It was custom-made for a pair of friendly cats that scamper
up and down it with ease.

Guests are given their own keys to the gate along with their room
keys; all rooms are entered from the patio. The rooms have contemporary furnishings, and all are impeccably clean, well maintained,
and comfortable. Each has air conditioning and heat and a private
entrance. Mrs. Underwood includes such extra amenities as a
morning paper "delivered silently" to guests' doors and her helpful,
privately printed brochure with recommendations on restaurants,
night spots, snacking places, walking tours, and such area services as
taxis and limousine service, as well as special places off the beaten

track. Near to all the French Quarter has to offer, the house is next to the 1734 Ursuline convent and across from another historic shrine, the Beauregard House. Early-morning and late-night snacks can be obtained at the old French Market just around the corner.

Accommodations: 7 rooms with private bath. *Pets:* Well-behaved pets permitted. *Children:* under thirteen not permitted. *Driving Instructions:* The French Quarter Maisonnettes are in the heart of the French Quarter, on Chartres Street between Ursuline and Governor Nichols streets.

HOTEL MAISON DE VILLE

727 Toulouse Street, New Orleans, LA 70130. 504-561-5858; toll free: 800-634-1600 (out of state). *Innkeeper:* Mark Duffy. Open all year.

The Hotel Maison de Ville is another world, devoted to comfort and service. Its guests are surrounded by furnishings that transport one immediately back to the court of France. Built sometime before 1742, the Maison appears on every existing early map of New Orleans. In the eighteenth century, its owner, A. A. Peychaud, concocted a mixed drink that included a dash of bitters. He stirred his invention with the quill of a cock, giving birth to the designation "cocktail." Tennessee Williams rewrote *A Streetcar Named Desire* on the hotel patio's wrought-iron tables. The original streetcar is on display in the French Market near the waterfront.

Near the brink of ruin not more than a dozen years ago, the Maison de Ville was saved through a heroic restoration by its new owners, Cornelius White and Terence Hall. The hotel—actually a collection of houses, most of which surround a New Orleans brick patio with a tiered central fountain—is bordered by palm trees. In addition to the Maison, there are four rooms in the converted slave quarters that were formerly connected but are now detached by a few steps. There is also a two-story suite that faces the patio; seven restored cottages operated by the Maison are about a block away. In one of these cottages, Audubon worked on most of the Louisiana portion of his "Birds of America" series.

It is possible to select almost any mood within the Maison's complex of buildings. The Audubon cottages offer an almost stark simplicity, with painted brick walls, exposed beam-and-plank ceilings, and slate or brick floors. This look of country elegance is enhanced by the Oriental rugs and carefully chosen antiques. Each cottage has a kitchen kept fully stocked with welcome items like a full array of mixers, butter, marmalade, and snacks, and each has its own private courtyard and faces the pool and cabana area. In the Maison itself, the feeling is a good deal more formal, with richly colored walls, French chairs and sofas, some bearing the original eighteenth-century needlepoint, marble fireplaces, gilt-framed mirrors, portraits of French gentlemen, and swagged drapes and matching quilted bed covers. The walls are painted in rich earth tones that establish the more formal mood of these quarters. The front door of the Maison is

an unusual example of etched-glass art.

A silver tray brings a breakfast of croissants, juice, and coffee, a sample of the Continental overtones pervading this French Quarter hotel. This is the only meal served, but the hotel's location near the finest restaurants in the South means that the best are but a few steps away. It is possible to walk over to Brennan's for breakfast, a New Orleans tradition and an orgy of eating pleasure. The expensiveness of Brennan's makes it an extravagance, but everyone should have quail to start the day at least once.

The Maison de Ville is one of the more expensive lodgings in New Orleans. It doesn't take long here to see why.

Accommodations: 21 rooms, 20 with private bath. Rates include breakfast and complimentary beverages such as sherry and port. *Pets:* Permitted in cottages only. *Driving Instructions:* The hotel is in the French Quarter between Bourbon and Royal on Toulouse Street.

LAFITTE GUEST HOUSE

1003 Bourbon Street, New Orleans, LA 70116. 504-581-2678.
Innkeeper: Steve Guyton. Open all year.

The Lafitte Guest House is a restored three-story brick French Quarter structure that was built in 1849 by P. G. Geleisses. On one side of the building, climbing vines have interwoven, almost obscuring the wall. On other sides, the brick is stuccoed in the fashion popular in the quarter. Typical New Orleans wrought ironwork decorates the second- and third-floor balconies on the front and side of the French Manor House.

Steve Guyton and his parents have carefully restored their guest house and decorated it with period antiques, paintings, and other Victoriana of all shapes and sizes. The velvet-draped parlor recalls the opulence of the Victorian age with red velvets, Oriental rugs, and lush plants. The mahogany mantle is not to be missed.

Many of the guest rooms have crystal chandeliers, typically six glass chimneys surrounding the candelabra bulbs. Furnishings include a blend of modern upholstered pieces and antiques mostly from the 1850–1900 period. Many of the rooms have the original black marble mantelpieces on the room fireplaces. All have coordinated swagged drapes and bedspreads in a variety of floral patterns. The bathrooms are tiled, and all rooms have carpeting, central air conditioning, and heating, as well as telephones. Five of the guest rooms are in the slave quarters opening onto the courtyard. Here the rooms are appealingly simple, with exposed brick walls and comfortable funishings. In the morning, a Continental breakfast of fresh juice, croissants, jam and butter, and coffee or tea is served. The inn offers free parking to guests, an unusual bonus with accommodations in the French Quarter.

Accommodations: 14 rooms with private bath. *Driving Instructions:* The guest house is on Bourbon Street, at the corner of Saint Phillip.

LAMOTHE HOUSE

621 Esplanade Avenue, New Orleans, LA 70116. 504-947-1161/ 1162. *Innkeepers:* Dr. and Mrs. Ralph Lupin; *Manager:* Susan Gonaux. Open all year.

Jean Lamothe knew the good life. As a wealthy sugar planter in the West Indies, he accustomed himself to surrounding his family with only the finest. In the early nineteenth century an insurrection at Santo Domingo forced the family to seek refuge in New Orleans, which was enjoying opulence thanks to a lion's share of the shipping trade and control of the surrounding plantations. Lamothe constructed one of the area's early double townhouses of brick, probably kilned nearby, although some of the French Quarter houses were built of brick brought down the Mississippi on barges.

As was the fashion, Lamothe built his house with a porte cochere, or carriageway, directly through the center of the house, leading to a central courtyard. The house has cypress floorboards and ceiling timbers that were hand-hewn, and many of its original hand-wrought iron fastenings on the doors and windows are in use today. In 1860, the four hand-carved Corinthian columns were added to the double entrance, and the porte cochere became the main hallway, leading to the twin winding stairways to the second-floor reception area and third-floor suites. The courtyard, made private by closing the porte cochere, is paved with flagstones that were originally a ship's ballast. The courtyard is flanked by the twin service wings that now offer accommodations in rooms once occupied by the house servants.

Like the other fine small hotels in the French Quarter, the Lamothe House has high ceilings and formal furniture. A complimentary breakfast is served in the dining room, and afternoon wine is set out in the parlor.

Lamothe House is decorated as befits Mr. Lamothe's original wealth. Special rooms are the Lafayette Suite and the Mallard Suite, named for one of the most respected nineteenth-century cabinet-makers in the city. Each piece in this room is a collector's item, and the decorative plaster cornicing is among the nicest in the city. The Lafayette Suite is equally distinguished with its pair of canopied four-poster beds, ornate armoire, marble-top dressers, and decorative plaster work. All guest rooms are decorated with Victorian antiques and have private baths, air-conditioning, and nightly turn-down service. Lamothe House is one of a handful of French Quarter hotels that have retained the ambience of an era gone by.

Accommodations: 20 rooms with private bath. *Pets:* Not permitted. *Driving Instructions:* The inn is on Esplanade Avenue between Royal and Chartres streets, at the eastern boundary of the French Quarter.

PARK VIEW GUEST HOUSE

7004 St. Charles Avenue, New Orleans, LA 70118. 504-861-7564.
Innkeeper: Zafer B. Zaitoon. Open all year.

Park View Guest House is in a quiet section of New Orleans overlooking Audubon Park. The St. Charles streetcar, the oldest operating streetcar line in the world runs right past the Park View on its way to downtown New Orleans and the night life of the Vieux Carre. The historic hotel, built as such for the World Cotton Exchange Exposition of 1885, is listed in the National Register of Historic Places. The twenty-five-room Victorian inn has three stories of verandas and balconies overlooking the park and its ancient live oaks. The elegant accoutrements are still here: Leaded and stained glass windows, transoms, and doors; crystal chandeliers; and antiques of a scale befitting the hotel's high-ceilinged rooms. Continental breakfasts of hot croissants and assorted jellies — the only meal at the inn — are served in the Audubon Room, but all of New Orlean's restaurants are but a 60¢ streetcar ride away.

Accommodations: 25 rooms, 10 with private bath. *Pets:* Not permitted. *Driving Instructions:* From I-10 take Carrollton exit to St. Charles. The inn is across from Tulane University and at the edge of Audubon Park.

THE SONIAT HOUSE

1133–37 Chartres Street, New Orleans, LA 70116. 504-522-0570. *Innkeeper:* Marc Turk. Open all year.

The Soniat House recently underwent a million-dollar renovation. It is actually two historic town houses joined by a carriageway leading to a common courtyard. One of the houses was built in 1830 by Joseph Soniat du Fossat, a wealthy planter who owned the Tchoupitoulas Plantation farther up the Mississippi. His town house is a fine example of the Creole-American style of architecture at the time of the

Louisiana Purchase. In the 1860s an elaborate cast-iron balcony of intricate grape-and-leaf clusters was added. Although less is known of the second town house, it is believed to have been built at about the same time as Soniat's and may be the work of the same architect.

All the guest rooms and suites are decorated with antique Oriental carpets, imported wall coverings, and unusual fabrics, which set off the hotel's collection of period antiques. Many of the rooms open onto balconies overlooking the landscaped courtyard, with its bower of wisteria, bougainvillea, sweet olive, jasmine, and banana trees. Complimentary breakfasts of juice, Creole coffee, and Southern biscuits arrive on a silver tray at guests' doors. Among the many amenities at the Soniat House are valet parking, Jacuzzis, telephones in both bedrooms and bathrooms, imported soaps, and thick, fluffy towels. On weekday mornings, limousine service to the business district is available. The Soniat House is in the heart of the Vieux Carré, minutes from its historic sights, fine restaurants, jazz clubs, and shops.

Accommodations: 25 rooms and suites, all with private bath. *Driving Instructions:* Leave I-10 East on Esplanade Avenue and take Esplanade to Decatur Street. Turn right, and go a few blocks to Ursuline. Turn right again, and go one block to Chartres Street. Turn right once more; the inn will be in the middle of the next block.

COTTAGE PLANTATION

U.S. 61, Saint Francisville, Louisiana. Mailing address: Route 5, Box 425, Saint Francisville, LA 70775. 504-635-3674. *Innkeepers:* Mr. & Mrs. Harvey Brown. Open all year except Christmas.

The Cottage Plantation is quite deservedly in the National Register of Historic Places. The property is located in the West Feliciana Parish, part of the "Garden of Louisiana," which contains one of the largest collections of antebellum plantation buildings anywhere. The mansion is actually a museum that graciously takes in overnight guests.

The land was acquired by a Spanish grant in 1795, and when Judge Butler — whose aristocratic family had been called Honor's Band by George Washington in honor of its military exploits — purchased the property in 1811, it was named China Trees after the long rows of Chinese-fern trees along the red clay bluff. The plantation house is at the end of Cottage Lane, a ¾-mile-long path that winds through the peaceful woodland off the highway. It is surrounded by a parklike setting with moss-draped shade trees and two English gardens containing japonicas and azaleas. The house was built in three sections, the first in 1795 and the last two in 1810 and 1850. The original section is Spanish in style with spacious rooms opening through French doors onto deep porches (or galleries, as they are called in Louisiana). The doorways are topped with delicate fretwork in gracefully arched transoms. The entire cottage is built of hand-hewn cypress, except for the thick 16- by 16-inch sills of poplar. All the woodwork is well crafted, inside and out. Every room has a hand-carved mantel, some with sunbursts and fluted Doric columns. Museum pieces and family heirlooms fill the house and blend with the original wall-coverings and Brussels carpets to add to the antebellum ambience. Here are hand-carved sideboards that display rare glass and china pieces, luxurious furniture of rosewood and mahogany, some with their original brocade upholstery, and large armoires and canopied bedsteads with lacy valances.

Guests at the plantation have the opportunity to sample life as it was lived on a luxurious Southern estate before the Civil War. The guest rooms have antique furnishings and decor as well as television, air conditioning, and central heating. A wake-up pot of coffee is

brought to rooms at 8 A.M.; later, a Southern breakfast of eggs, grits, hot biscuits, and bacon is served in the main dining room. This is followed by a tour of the house, grounds, and outbuildings, including the original schoolhouse, slave quarters, milk house, outside kitchen, carriage and horse barns, and Judge Butler's law offices. The plantation has furnishings, diaries, mementos, and correspondence of the influential Butler family, including letters from some of the most prestigious figures in American history. Beyond the cottage and the outbuildings lie pastures, an ancient orchard, and a tiny cemetery. Tours of the Cottage Plantation are open to the public, and the old kitchen now contains a gift-antique shop. There is a swimming pool for guests.

Accommodations: 6 rooms with private bath. *Pets:* Not permitted. *Driving Instructions:* The Cottage Plantation is 6 miles north of Saint Francisville off U.S. 61 on Cottage Lane, which is the driveway of the plantation.

GLENCOE PLANTATION

Route 68, Wilson, Louisiana. Mailing address: P.O. Box 178, Wilson, LA 70789. 504-629-5387. *Innkeeper:* W. Jerome Westerfield, Jr. Open all year.

Glencoe is in the heart of "plantation country," surrounded by 1,038 acres of rolling hills with landscaped grounds and gardens of azaleas, camellias, myrtles, and magnolias. Century-old live oaks shade the lawns. The original plantation house was built in 1870, but it burned down in 1898. The present turreted, gingerbreaded manor house, erected in 1903 on the same foundation, is considered one of the finest examples of Queen Anne–style Victorian Gothic in Louisiana. The rooms are furnished and decorated in keeping with the turn of the century. Each of the four guest rooms in the main house opens onto a gingerbreaded porch complete with comfortable old rocking chairs. Eight other guest rooms are in Victorian-style cottages of recent vintage. Each of these has king-size beds and Victorian appointments. Guests are welcome to explore the plantation and use the swimming, fishing, and hiking facilities, as well as the lighted tennis court. Breakfast is served to overnight guests, and other meals are available to guests and the public by advance reservation.

Accommodations: 12 rooms with private bath. *Pets:* Not permitted. *Driving Instructions:* Take U.S. 61 north from Baton Rouge. Turn onto Route 68 and drive 15½ miles north.

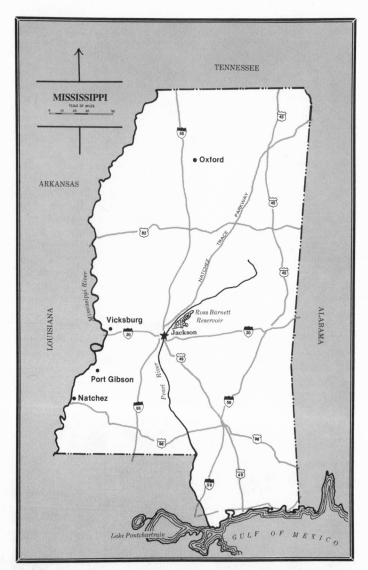

Mississippi

Natchez, Mississippi

THE BURN

712 North Union Street, Natchez, MS 39120. 601-445-8566 or 442-1344. *Innkeepers:* Mayor and Mrs. Tony Byrne. Open all year.

The antebellum South waits, alive and well, in Natchez, Mississippi. The Burn was built in 1832 by John Walworth, a passenger on a steamboat down the Mississippi to New Orleans. When the boat docked in Natchez, Walworth decided to stroll through the town to have a look around. He never left.

Walworth built his home in classic Greek Revival style. The overhung second floor forms the roof of the front porch, which is supported by four fluted Greek columns. Gardens slope away from the home on all sides, with more than one hundred and twenty-five varieties of camellias and other shrubs and flowers. The herb garden, with the oldest fountain in Natchez, faces the Garçonnièrre, a guest house. The Burn, Scottish for "brook," was named by Walworth after the stream that passed through the property. Ironically, The Burn did suffer a fire shortly after it was built, and the second floor was rebuilt in the style that survives today. During the Civil War, the house was used as headquarters by Federal troops and later became a hospital for Union soldiers.

Today, The Burn contains a priceless collection of eighteenth- and nineteenth-century antiques. It has a semispiral, unsupported stair-

way in the front entrance hall. On the wall is a gilt-framed mirror, just one of a number of mirrors throughout the house. A fine crystal chandelier, also one of many, hangs at the foot of the stairs. The Burn has a collection of furniture and accessories any museum would be proud of, but these antiques are part of the house and are used. Upstairs is a huge canopy bed that has been attributed to a renowned New Orleans cabinetmaker. There are dozens of Empire and earlier chairs, dressers, armoires, and sofas. Many of the rugs are Aubusson; the draperies were imported from Belgium. Each lighting fixture is a carefully wired original piece.

Overnight guests are given rooms in the main house and Garçonnière, where among the furnishings there is an acanthus-carved four-poster canopy bed covered by an antique hand-crocheted spread. Each of the rooms has a private bath, air-conditioner, and television. The downstairs parlor and informal dining room are where the guests gather for fellowship and Southern hospitality. A plantation breakfast is served to all guests, and dinner is available on request.

Accommodations: 6 rooms with private bath. *Children:* Only school-age. *Pets:* Not permitted. *Driving Instructions:* From the center of town, take State, Franklin, High, or Madison streets to Union Street, then take Union to The Burn, which is between B and Oak streets.

LINDEN

Melrose Avenue, Natchez, MS 39120. 601-445-5472. *Innkeeper:* Jeanette S. Feltus. Open all year.

Linden is an outstanding example of antebellum architecture. The imposing portico across the entire length of the mansion, the balustraded upper gallery, and the parklike grounds of oaks and cedars dripping Spanish moss all work a powerful magic that instantly transports visitors back to a more genteel era. The elegant Federal-style mansion, built in three sections between 1790 and 1849, has been the residence of one family for six generations. Jeanette Feltus and her family still live here, opening their home to overnight visitors.

Houseguests are surrounded by the grandeur of a wealthy cotton merchant's eighteenth-century home. Many of the pieces in the home are family heirlooms dating from the eighteenth and nineteenth centuries and brought here from all over the world. Guest rooms are furnished with canopied four-poster beds set on fine Persian carpets. Their walls are decorated with rare prints and oil paintings, and on display are Chinese porcelains and French crystal.

Guests are served a breakfast of homemade biscuits, eggs, and ham and grits and then given a tour of the house. Jeanette Feltus loves Linden and certainly knows its history and even its secrets. Lucky houseguests hear stories of the many escapades of resident ghosts.

Accommodations: 5 rooms with private bath. *Pets:* Not permitted. *Children:* Under ten not permitted. *Driving Instructions:* Linden is in the historic district of Natchez, off Melrose Avenue.

MONMOUTH PLANTATION

Corner of Melrose Avenue and John A. Quitman Parkway, Natchez, Mississippi. Mailing address: P.O. Box 1736, Natchez, MS 39120. 601-442-5852. Open all year.

There is no better way to get the feeling of the opulent life-style of an antebellum Mississippi plantation than to stay at a Natchez mansion, and certainly none has been more handsomely restored than the *circa*-1818 former home of John A. Quitman. Quitman, a governor of Mississippi and later a U.S. congressman from Adams County, purchased Monmouth for his bride, Eliza, in 1826. Today the stately, columned mansion is a veritable museum of Civil War memorabilia, as well as many personal items from the Quitman collection, including the gold sword presented to Quitman by President Polk in honor of his brave leadership of troops during the war with Mexico. Listed in the National Register of Historic Places, Monmouth Plantation is open daily to visitors, and overnight guests may tour the mansion without charge. The John Quitman Room, where guests may stay, has an oversize four-poster, a velvet swagged tester, Oriental carpeting,

oil paintings, and a decorative but nonworking fireplace. It should be noted that this room is part of the house tour; so guests who wish to use their room during the day will probably be happier in any of the other guest rooms. These rooms all have canopied beds, antique armoires, air conditioning, private telephones, cable television, and wall-to-wall carpeting. Some rooms have a small antique writing desk, two chairs, and a chest of drawers. Except for the John Quitman Room, which is in the mansion itself, all are in what were originally the slave quarters, a brick building that could stand alone as a country inn. A full breakfast is served to overnight guests in the original slave kitchen, which is furnished as it was in 1840, and cocktails and hors d'oeuvres are served in the late afternoon. Surrounding the mansion are 26 acres of grounds, which guests are free to explore.

Accommodations: 11 rooms with private bath. *Pets:* Not permitted. *Children:* Under ten not permitted. *Driving Instructions:* The plantation is a mile east of the center of Natchez.

SILVER STREET INN

1 Silver Street, Natchez, Mississippi. Mailing address: P.O. Box 1224, Natchez, MS 39120. 601-442-4221. *Innkeeper:* Lu Barraza. Open all year.

The Silver Street Inn is an 1840s wood-framed building on a cliff overlooking the mighty Mississippi River. A fairly colorful imagination is needed to conjure up this tidy, quaint little inn's past. Everything is so pristine and proper these days, with rag rugs on polished bare-wood floors, painted iron beds color-coordinated with the floral-print wallpapers and quilts. But in the wild and woolly days of riverboat gamblers just off the paddle wheelers, the inn was a well-known house of ill repute. Today all that is left of its bawdy past is a collection of tales and "Madame," an almost life-size doll who greets visitors in the hall.

The Silver Street Inn has been restored and decorated under the watchful eyes of her innkeepers, who also run the dress shop on the ground floor. The inn itself occupies the second story of the building. Several rooms overlook the river where Mississippi paddle wheelers still dock on cruises out of New Orleans. The upper veranda is lined with rockers, and guests frequently gather there to watch the evening sun go down over the river. The living room is a popular spot, with its working fireplaces and attractive Mississippi antique pieces. No meals are served.

Accommodations: 4 rooms, 2 with private bath. *Driving Instructions:* The inn is on Silver Street in Natchez-under-the-Hill, alongside the Mississippi River.

THE OLIVER-BRITT HOUSE INN AND TEA ROOM

512 Van Buren Avenue, Oxford, MS 38655. 600-234-8043. *Innkeepers:* Larry and Mary Ann Britt, Ernest and Glynn Oliver. Open all year.

Oxford and its environs were the inspiration for William Faulkner, whose mythical Yoknapatawpa County sprang from his lifetime knowledge of the region. Faulkner's Oxford home, Rowan Oak, attracts scholars and visitors from around the world. Oxford is also home to the University of Mississippi and a handsome Greek Revival manor, The Oliver-Britt House.

This bed-and-breakfast inn is the creation of Glynn Oliver and Mary Ann Britt, who transformed the 1905 building into a popular tearoom and overnight lodging. The front of the inn has eight columns supporting two stories of classic Southern verandas, complete with cane-bottom rocking chairs and enhanced by tidy border gardens and shade trees. The five guest rooms offer a variety of antique, canopied, or oversized brass beds, along with ceiling fans, color television, fresh flowers, and coordinated linens, curtains, and bedcovers. Overnight guests are served a full breakfast, and lunches are available to the public Mondays through Fridays. On special college weekends, dinners are often served as well. A favorite luncheon dish is the innkeepers' chicken salad made with their own pickles and accompanied by their popular strawberry bread.

Mary Ann and Glynn will help guests plan the day's outings. Historic Oxford Square is within walking distance, with its many shops and restaurants.

Accommodations: 5 rooms with private bath. *Driving Instructions:* From Memphis take I-55 south to Batesville and Mississippi Route 6 east 25 miles to Oxford. Stay on the bypass and take the second exit, Old Taylor Road, left to the end. Turn right. Take the first left and go to the end. Turn right. The inn is the second building on the right.

Port Gibson, Mississippi

OAK SQUARE

1207 Church Street, Port Gibson, MS 39150. 601-437-4350 or 601-437-5771. *Innkeepers:* Martha B. and William D. Lum. Open all year.

General Ulysses S. Grant once said that Port Gibson was "too beautiful to burn." It is fortunate he felt that way, because Port Gibson has survived as one of the state's most historic towns.

Named in honor of the many tall oaks on its grounds, this mansion is distinguished by its six 22-foot Corinthian columns imported from England and topped with terra-cotta capitals. Inside, a wide entry hall leads to a graceful staircase ascending to a columned landing, where it separates into twin stairways that continue to the second floor. The double parlor has an 1850 carved rosewood Victorian parlor suite with matching sofas, center tables, and French Rococo Revival pier and mantel mirrors. A rare Chickering piano is the focal point of the library, which is furnished with Empire and Victorian pieces.

Accommodations are in the Guest House, in rooms with furnishings like those in Oak Square. In one, a bed has four heavy turned posts that rise 7 feet to a pleated canopy. A Victorian love seat is at the foot of the bed. A complete Southern breakfast and a tour of the mansion are included with overnight accommodations.

Accommodations: 10 guest rooms and suites, all with private bath. *Pets:* A kennel is available nearby. *Driving Instructions:* Port Gibson is 40 miles north of Natchez on Route 61.

Vicksburg, Mississippi

ANCHUCA

 1010 First East, Vicksburg, MS 39180. 601-636-4931. *Innkeepers:* May and Martin White. Open all year.

Just a few brick-paved streets away from the Mississippi River, in the heart of Vicksburg's historic district, is the Anchuca mansion. The main section of the house was built in 1830, with an imposing facade; and another story was added in 1845. This face-lift was considered rather "pretentious" in its day, although it must have appealed to Jefferson Davis, who made a speech from the new balcony during the Civil War.

 Today the mansion has been restored to its antebellum elegance,

complete with gas-burning crystal chandeliers, Oriental rugs, and lavish period furnishings. The original slave quarters have been transformed into guest rooms filled with formal antiques including large four-poster or half-tester beds. Two rooms have gas-burning fireplaces, and one of these has its fireplace in its bathroom. A turn-of-the-century cottage houses additional guest rooms. On the brick patio there are both a swimming pool and a glass-enclosed hot tub for year-round use. A Southern breakfast is the only meal served in the formal dining room.

Accommodations: 9 rooms with private bath. *Driving Instructions:* In Vicksburg take Clay Street to Cherry Street and turn right. Go five blocks to First East and turn right again.

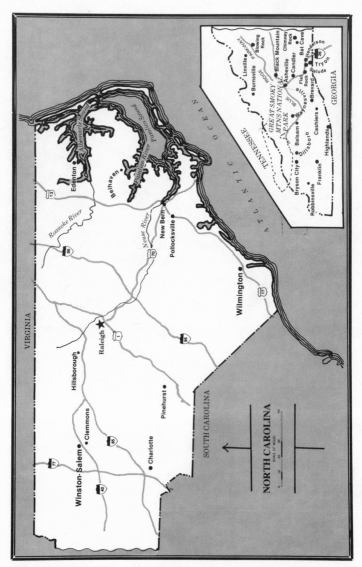

North Carolina

Asheville, North Carolina

FLINT STREET INN

116 Flint Street, Asheville, NC 28801. 704-253-6723. *Innkeepers:*
Rick and Lynne Vogel. Open all year.

The Flint Street Inn is a 1915 home on a half acre of dogwood, oak,
and mountain laurel in the historic Montford district of Asheville. A
flower garden and a lily pond are in the yard. The house, listed in the
National Register of Historic Places, has been restored in keeping
with the early twentieth century and furnished much as it would have
been in the 1920s and 1930s, including beautifully preserved overstuffed couches and chairs in the living room. A variety of Art
Nouveau and Art Deco pieces are displayed, as well as a large collection of wooden clocks, all of which are in working order. Guests enjoy
discovering the little personal touches throughout the inn. One guest
room has a hand-crocheted bedspread, and in another, Lynne's
grandmother's hat collection is hung up over the antique dressing

table. A 1920s dress hangs in the closet of a third. The aroma of freshly baked muffins or biscuits starts the day off. A Southern-style breakfast is served in the old-fashioned dining room or out on the spacious front veranda. The inn is centrally located just a few blocks from downtown Asheville and its restored shopping areas and Civic Center.

Accommodations: 4 rooms, 2 with private bath. *Pets and children:* Not permitted. *Driving Instructions:* Take the I-240 bypass and exit onto Haywood Street. Continue to Flint Street several blocks north of the city.

THE OLD REYNOLDS MANSION

100 Reynolds Heights, Asheville, NC 28804. 704-254-0496. *Innkeepers:* Fred and Helen Faber. Open all year.

As was so often the case in the last century, the Old Reynolds Mansion was built gradually over a period of years. The first section was built before the Civil War, while the third floor and porches were added early in this century. The result of this gradual expansion is a seventeen-room, three-story brick mansion on 4 acres in a country setting.

Refurbishing and decorating a home of this size has been a challenge for the Fabers, who first came to the mountain region in the early 1970s and have been working on their restoration project for more than a decade. Completed now, their home reflects Helen's decorating skills and the couple's enthusiasm for antique collecting. Wide stairways and halls have been papered with old-fashioned prints. Many windows offer views of the mountains, and the four rooms on the second floor have working fireplaces. There is also a working fireplace in the breakfast room, where guests enjoy their morning juice, coffee, and rolls. Outside, a large swimming pool built in the 1930s is surrounded by pine trees.

Accommodations: 10 rooms, 3 with private bath. *Pets:* Not permitted. *Driving Instructions:* Take Merrimon Avenue (Route 25 north) past Beaver Lake, turn right just past the stop light onto Beaver Street, and turn left up the gravel lane to the inn.

THE RAY HOUSE BED AND BREAKFAST

83 Hillside Street, Asheville, NC 28801. 704-252-0106. *Innkeepers:* Alice and Will Curtis. Open all year.

Sometime during the 1890s, Captain John Ray built this Colonial-revival home for his family. It features a wraparound porch and handsome windows and woodwork. The feeling at The Ray House is entirely English. In fact, according to innkeeper Alice Curtis, one English guest said it reminded her of the William Morris House near Oxford, England. The Ray House is furnished with a mixture of antique and reproduction pieces. Guests may use the beamed living room and the library–music room downstairs. A Continental breakfast is served in the dining room, on the porch, or in the garden.

Three guest rooms are named for famous Asheville citizens. The Thomas Wolfe Room overlooks the side garden and an ancient Japanese maple. Its bath has a built-in bookcase with books of local lore as well as paperback novels. The O. Henry Room is furnished with twin walnut spool beds, and the Bartok Room has a view of the side yard and is decorated with country-French wallpaper.

Accommodations: 3 rooms, 1 with private bath. *Pets:* Not permitted. *Driving Instructions:* From I-240, take the Merrimon Avenue exit, then take Merrimon Avenue (Route 25) north. Go to the second traffic light and turn left onto Hillside. Ray House is on the corner of Hillside and Mount Clare.

BALSAM LODGE BED AND BREAKFAST

Box 279, Balsam, NC 28707. 704-456-6528. *Innkeeper:* Marie E. Pike. Open June through October.

On a hillside in the Great Smoky Mountains, there is a peaceful little vacation spot, the Balsam Lodge, incorporating two early 1900s buildings, one a yellow-clapboard farmhouse furnished with antiques, the other a red-and-white railroad depot moved here from the town by innkeepers Marie and Gordon Pike. The depot houses several efficiency apartments with a deck overlooking the mountains. The house has several cozy bedrooms and a living room where guests gather for Marie's breakfasts of homemade breads, muffins, and biscuits, set out along with pots of her jams and jellies and fresh seasonal fruits. Evenings are cooled by mountain breezes. It is then that guests often return to the living room to visit by the fireside over a cup of coffee and some of Marie's special treats. The porch, with its rockers and an old-fashioned swing, is another favorite with guests. The grounds are home to many varieties of birds and flowers, and there is a goldfish pond, complete with a waterwheel.

Accommodations: 8 rooms, 4 with private bath. *Pets:* Permitted in depot only. *Driving Instructions:* Take Route 19A-23 (Smoky Mountain Expressway) 7½ miles. The lodge is approximately ¼ mile off the main highway in Balsam, 35 miles west of Asheville.

BALSAM MOUNTAIN INN

Routes 19A and 23, Balsam, North Carolina. Mailing address: P.O. Box 40, Balsam, NC 28707. 704-456-9498. *Innkeepers:* Donald and Elizabeth, Robert and Sara LaBrant. Open June 15 through Labor Day.

The Balsam Mountain Inn in the Smoky Mountains sits high on shaded lawns and boasts two stories of spacious verandas across its entire length. Groupings of antique wicker rockers and old "Papa bear" chairs line the porches. Twenty-six acres of mountain woodland envelop the inn, built in 1906. Time seems to have stopped here, and the inn offers the same restful lawn games offered to previous generations. There is shuffleboard, croquet, and acres of grounds to stroll on. The lobby still has its oaken coatracks, pine rockers, and loads of old wicker chairs and occasional tables. Most of its furnishings were here when the inn opened. The antique box-case pendulum clock still ticks away from its perch on the lobby wall, and old-fashioned braided and hooked rugs are scattered on the bare hardwood floors of the bright and airy room. Guests can usually find a good game of cards going on here.

The guest rooms, on the first and second floors, are located off the long hallways designed to accommodate the steamer trunks of long-ago visitors. The wide halls are lined with old prints and furnishings. Guest rooms—sunny and bright, with floral-patterned wallpapers, iron bedsteads painted white to match the white bureaus, and oak-framed mirrors—have views of the surrounding Smoky mountains.

Breakfasts and dinners are served in the dining room with its white napery and groupings of the inn's original bent-wood chairs. A large mirrored sideboard oversees the room, and drapes are pulled back to let the fresh mountain air in through the tall windows. Meals are served family style, with waitresses bringing heaping platters of "home-cooked" food to individual tables. After guests have helped themselves at the salad bar, the meal begins. Only one entrée is offered, along with large helpings of five or six fresh vegetables picked that day. Fresh flowers grace the dining room and lobby, adding color and fragrance to the pleasant vacation atmosphere.

The innkeepers have run the inn since the 1960s. Donald and Elizabeth care for the guest rooms and lobby, and their son Robert and his wife Sara are in charge of the dining room and kitchen. Helping them are several kinfolk and the gardener and housekeeper, who are almost part of the family. This is a well-loved country inn in one of the most beautiful spots in the East.

Accommodations: 37 rooms, 30 with private bath. *Pets:* Not permitted. *Driving Instructions:* Go 7 miles west of Waynesville on Route 19A-23. The inn is ¼ mile off the main highway in Balsam.

Bat Cave, North Carolina

STONEHEARTH INN

Route 74, Bat Cave, North Carolina. Mailing address: P.O. Box 9, Bat Cave, NC 28710. 704-625-9990. *Innkeepers:* Don and Ellen Staley. Open all year.

How could anyone resist investigating an inn in a town called Bat Cave? The Stonehearth Inn sits beside the Rocky Broad River in that valley town. Built in 1940, it is a comfortable country place surrounded by the wilderness of the Blue Ridge Mountains. The inn's guest rooms have a rustic look, with their wood-paneled walls; simple, mountain-style furnishings; and handmade dust ruffles on the beds. The Rocky Broad River, named for the water-smoothed boulders in its bed, lulls guests to sleep. Its tree-shaded waters flow past the inn.

In the dining room, ruffled curtains, calico tablecloths, and a fire in the large stone hearth add to the inn's Blue Ridge atmosphere. All-you-can-eat menus are the highlight Tuesday through Saturday, the days the restaurant is open in season (April through December). There is usually a choice of eight entrées each evening, with Ellen Staley's specialties including fried chicken and rainbow trout prepared five different ways. The Staleys serve guests a Continental breakfast, and the public is welcome at dinner.

Accommodations: 4 rooms with private bath. *Pets:* Not permitted. *Driving Instructions:* From Asheville, to the north, take I-40 to Route 74 and go about 20 miles to Bat Cave. From Lake Lure and Chimney Rock, take Route 74 west 3 to 5 miles.

Belhaven, North Carolina

RIVER FOREST MANOR

    600 East Main Street, Belhaven, NC 27810. 919-943-2151.
Innkeepers: Melba G. Smith, Mark C. Smith, and Axson Smith,
Jr. Open all year.

The year was 1899, and John Aaron Wilkinson had decided to build
himself a mansion befitting his station as president of the Roper Lumber Company and vice-president of the Norfolk and Southern Railroad. Known for his uncompromising attention to detail, he hired a
team of skilled Italian craftsmen to carve the ornate ceilings and oak
mantels, and to fit cut glass into the leaded windows. The result was
the largest home in Belhaven, for many years an important social
center. The mansion survived intact and is today the River Forest

Manor. Purchased in 1947 by Axson Smith, who managed it until his death in 1979, the inn is now managed by his wife, Melba, and son, Axson, Jr. Still here are the crystal chandeliers installed by Wilkinson, the mahogany wainscoting and tapestries, and two baths so large they include bathtubs for two. Of the manor's eleven fireplaces, five are in guest rooms and still functioning. One walks through a grove of long-needle pines and up steps through an impressive entrance flanked by six two-story Ionic columns, to enter a house clearly of another era. The bedrooms upstairs all contain Victorian furniture, and the feeling is one of elegance, Southern style.

Jacuzzis and tennis courts are available, but many guests come to River Forest Manor solely for its food. The 75-dish smorgasbord brings guests from miles around. Among its special treasures are hush puppies, oyster fritters, shrimp creole, crabmeat casserole, home-made sausage, corn bread, roast ham and turkey, and an assortment of freshly baked desserts. The list of selections seems almost endless, and guests may refill their plates as often as they wish.

Because of the River Forest's location on the Intracoastal Waterway, guests may arrive by boat as well as by car. The River Forest Yacht Club offers sixteen-hour dock service, and marine services.

Accommodations: 12 rooms with private bath. Some are in an adjacent motel section; be sure to specify which you prefer. *Pets:* Not permitted. *Driving Instructions:* Belhaven is 30 miles east of Washington, North Carolina, on Route 264.

Black Mountain, North Carolina

THE RED ROCKER INN

136 North Dougherty Street, Black Mountain, NC 28711. 704-669-5991. *Innkeepers:* Pat and Fred Eshleman. Open May through October.

Black Mountain sits at the edge of the Great Smoky Mountains, just a short drive from Asheville, the Blue Ridge Parkway, and Mount Mitchell — at 6,684 feet, the tallest mountain east of the Mississippi River. The Red Rocker Inn is a family resort on one of the Black Mountain area's highest knobs, just a few blocks from town. The main section was built in 1894 by Silas Dougherty as a wedding gift to his daughter. A wing was added twenty years later.

Pat and Fred Eshleman took over the inn in the early 1980s, restoring it to its turn-of-the-century look with Victorian antiques. Guests often gather around the player piano in the living room, and a game room has a selection of books and games for evenings and rainy days. Meals are served in the red-and-white dining room, which has three working fireplaces. Guests may dine together around large circular tables that seat twelve or at more intimate tables for one or two couples. The specialties of the house are the Southern pan-fried chicken, fresh mountain trout, beef ribs, and chicken saltimbocca. All meals are available and are served both to guests and the public. A line of rocking chairs is set up on the veranda outside.

Accommodations: 18 rooms, 12 with private bath, and 2 suites. *Pets:* Not permitted. *Driving Instructions:* From I-40 take the Black Mountain exit and drive to the center of town. Turn left, turn right after one block, and proceed to the top of the hill.

Blowing Rock, North Carolina

RAGGED GARDEN INN AND RESTAURANT

Sunset Drive, Blowing Rock, North Carolina. Mailing address: P.O. Box 1927, Blowing Rock, NC 28605. 704-295-9703. *Innkeepers:* Joyce and Joe Villani. Open mid-April through December.

Ragged Gardens, built at the turn of the century as a summer home, is surrounded by terraced rose gardens, dogwoods, azaleas, rhododendrons, and apple trees. The building has a stone-columned entrance, and its exterior is covered with chestnut bark slabs. Inside, the inn has an unusual slate and stone staircase. Several walls have dark, floor-to-ceiling wood paneling, and an interesting collection of antique ceiling fixtures has been installed throughout. The four guest rooms upstairs have wall-to-wall carpeting, comforters, and papered or painted walls with contrasting trim. Restaurateur Joe Villani, no stranger to the business, first worked at Sardi's in Manhattan, then owned The Gaslight in Greenwich, Connecticut, and later La Belle Verrière in Winter Park, Florida, and the Driftwood in Vero Beach. His classic French and Northern Italian cuisine at the Ragged Garden includes linguine al pesto, cannelloni alla Bolognese, saltinbocca alla Romana, osso bucco, and filet mignon Bordelaise. Breakfast is for guests only.

Accommodations: 3 rooms and 1 suite, all with private bath. *Pets and children under 13:* Not permitted. *Driving Instructions:* Take Route 321 into Blowing Rock. Turn west at the light onto Sunset Drive and go up the hill to the inn, across from the school.

Brevard, North Carolina

THE INN AT BREVARD

410 East Main Street, Brevard, NC 28712. 704-884-2105. *Innkeepers:* Bertrand and Eileen Bourget. Open all year except a short period in winter.

The Inn at Brevard was built at the turn of the century as a private home for William Breese and his family. Breese, once the mayor of Brevard and later a state senator, was a prominent attorney who in 1911 hosted a reunion of the troops who had served under Stonewall Jackson.

Today The Inn at Brevard consists of two buildings. The main inn, listed in the National Register of Historic Places, is old-fashioned, with lacy white curtains at the windows and period wall coverings. Throughout the inn you will find original brass hardware, carved fireplaces, and turn-of-the-century furnishings.

Two guest rooms have been restored in this building. One has a brass bed, a braided oval rug, and an Empire dresser with matching mirror. Ten additional rooms are in a separate three-story building facing a quiet side street. Rooms there are paneled, and most have Victorian pieces. All have television and private baths. A full breakfast is served to the public, lunch and dinner on Friday and Saturday only.

Accommodations: 12 rooms, 10 with private bath. *Pets:* Not permitted. *Driving Instructions:* Brevard is about 20 miles west of Hendersonville on Route 64.

FOLKESTONE LODGE

Route 1, West Deep Creek Road, Bryson City, North Carolina.
Mailing address: Route 1, P.O. Box 310, Bryson City, NC 28713.
704-488-2730. *Innkeepers:* Irene and Bob Kranich. Open May
through November.

Folkestone Lodge, an old-fashioned farmhouse-inn minutes from the
Deep Creek entrance to the Smoky Mountain National Park, has
been carefully preserved and restored by Irene and Bob Kranich. The
Kraniches painstakingly created private bathrooms for each of the
guest rooms, taking care to leave the stonework unharmed. The unusual bathrooms have old Victorian claw-footed tubs and antique
washstands. Some of the guest rooms and bathrooms have low
pressed-tin ceilings, antique wicker and dark wood furnishings, and
small stained-glass windows that swing open, reminiscent of an Old
World country *auberge*. Each room has its own special bedstead, one
an old sleigh bed, another a large oak Victorian. Each is covered with
an antique crocheted bedspread.

Oriental rugs and antique furnishings are placed throughout on
the lodge's stone floors, and bowls of fresh fruit and flowers welcome
guests. Big home-cooked breakfasts are served family-style in the
spacious dining room, where floor-to-ceiling windows provide
commanding views of the surrounding mountains. The meal comes
with plenty of freshly baked breads and is the perfect start to a day of

hiking and exploring. Irene and Bob are both avid lovers of the great outdoors and will gladly share their knowledge with interested visitors. The library is well stocked with books of mountain lore. The country setting is enhanced by a nearby mountain stream and natural rock bridges. A ten-minute walk leads to the Deep Creek Entrance of the park, where there are three crystal-clear waterfalls. Nearer home are old-time outdoor summer games including croquet and horseshoes. On rainy and chilly days and evenings, guests can join forces for a game of chess, checkers, or ping pong.

Accommodations: 5 rooms with private bath. *Children and Pets:* Children in very small numbers; and pets not at all. *Driving Instructions:* Follow road signs to Deep Creek Campground (national park facility). A Folkestone Lodge sign is on the left, about ⅛ mile from the campground. It is 2 miles from Bryson City to the Lodge.

FRYEMONT INN

Fryemont Road, Bryson City, North Carolina. *Mailing address:* Box 459, Bryson City, NC 28713. 704-488-2159. *Innkeepers:* Sue and George Brown. Open mid-April through October.

In the late nineteenth century Captain Amos Frye amassed a fortune from the timber empire he had established in the Great Smoky Mountains wilderness. When the bottom dropped out of the lumber business in 1921, he decided to build an inn to serve the many travelers who had begun to come to the mountains as a retreat from city life.

The handsome rustic lodge was constructed of chestnut, oak, and maple timbers felled by Frye's axmen throughout his forest acreage. Frye sought out the most talented mountain blacksmith to create the inn's iron hardware, and skillful masons built fireplaces large enough to burn logs 10 feet long. One such fireplace is in the inn's lobby; another is in the dining room, where cheese soup, country ham, fried chicken, and fresh mountain trout are among the regular offerings. Breads are baked fresh daily at Fryemont, as are all its pies and cakes. Breakfast is served.

Many of the inn's guest rooms are combination living rooms and bedrooms with wall-to-wall carpeting. Windows were fashioned from hand-hewn timbers, and bedroom walls are of wide boards cut from local trees.

Within a short drive from the Fryemont are the Museum of the Cherokee Indian, the Oconaluftee Indian village, and the outdoor

drama *Unto These Hills,* which tells the story of the Cherokee Indian. The nearby Great Smoky Mountains National Park is the most extensive wilderness east of the Mississippi. A big local attraction is whitewater rafting on the Nantahala River. The innkeepers can streer interested guests to the best spots and outfitters.

Accommodations: 37 rooms with private bath. *Pets:* Not permitted. *Driving Instructions:* Take the Bryson City exit off Route 19-A. Turn right exactly 0.3 mile up the paved road at the inn's sign.

RANDOLPH HOUSE

Fryemont Road, Bryson City, North Carolina. Mailing address: P.O. Box 816, Bryson City, NC 28713. 704-488-3472. *Innkeepers:* Bill and Ruth Randolph Adams. Open April to November.

In 1895, Attorney Amos Frye built what came to be known as the "Mansion on the Hill." At the time he and his wife, Lillian, owned thousands of acres in Bryson City, and the house was designed to be fitting for a man of such property. The many-gabled mansion contains a large dining room and seven bedrooms as well as many of the original furnishings installed by the Fryes and their daughter and son-in-law, Lois and John Randolph. Today it is run as a genteel country inn by John Randolph's niece and her husband; meals are prepared in the Southern tradition. The menu changes daily and always includes salad, homemade yeast rolls, local fresh vegetables, and dessert. Entrées are chosen from a long list of Ruth's specialties, including fried chicken, prime ribs with sautéed mushrooms, stuffed

mountain trout, and veal parmesan. Vegetables might be fresh string beans, squash casserole, or candied apples; the dessert of the day is often Key lime pie. Reservations are required of the public wishing to dine at the inn. A selection of mountain-made crafts, jellies, and honey is offered for sale. On warm nights guests often gather on the front porch with its country rockers; on winter evenings, a large open fireplace is kept blazing to dispel the chill.

Accommodations: 6 rooms, 3 with private bath. When all rooms are filled, all share baths. *Pets:* Not permitted. *Driving Instructions:* Take Route 19A (second exit) into Bryson City. Turn right at the historic sign and continue 1/10 mile to the Randolph House.

Burnsville, North Carolina

THE NU WRAY INN

P.O. Box 156, Burnsville, NC 28714. 704-682-2329. *Innkeeper:* Betty Souders. Open all year; dining room open May to December. At one time, an eight-room log cabin stood where the Nu Wray Inn now stands. The cabin, built in 1833, was enlarged into a full-scale country inn in 1867 by the grandfather of the current owner. The result is a Southern country inn reminiscent of many fine New England inns. It commands one end of the village square, watched over by the statue of Otway Burns. The town was named after Burns, the commander of the privateer "Snapdragon" in the War of 1812.

Having been in the same family for four generations, the Nu Wray has had time to collect and preserve a large number of antiques displayed or, more properly, used in a setting of early wallpapers and bright colonial colors. The parlor or Music Room of the inn has some of the more formal furniture, with early sofas and tufted Victorian chairs facing a grand piano in one corner. Music is clearly loved by the innkeeper, and the collection of instruments ranges from an 1830 rosewood square piano to player pianos to an early disc Reginaphone music box. The list might include even the carved cuckoo clock with its deer's head, bunnies, alpine horn, and crossed wooden rifles encircling the clock mechanism.

At the Nu Wray, the patina of time glows on an old one-armed school desk, a five-drawer chest, a deep-red harvest table, and a soft-pine hutch that holds the family collection of pressed glass and china. Some ceilings have modern tiles, but these are barely noticed in an inn that feels lived in and welcoming. As at all popular inns, it is advisable to reserve rooms in advance.

Family-style meals at long tables set with linen cloths or lace, reminiscent of grandmother's table, are served at the inn. Specialties are simple and to the point: heaps of hickory-smoked country ham or fried chicken and dressing, and plates of vegetables and salads, yams and greens, fresh tomatoes, and, of course, corn bread and baskets of buttery biscuits.

Accommodations: 35 rooms, 25 with private bath. *Pets:* Not permitted. *Driving Instructions:* Take U.S. 19 or 19E directly into the center of Burnsville. The inn is on the square. Reservations suggested.

Cashiers forms a backdrop to the several resorts dotting the country-side in this southwestern North Carolina community. To the north of the town, in Glenville, is *Thorpe Lake,* created by Thorpe Dam. The lake is a popular spot for fishing, boating, water-skiing, and swimming. This area is noted for its waterfalls, of which *Whitewater Falls,* with its double falls, heads the list. The upper falls cascade 411 feet, the greatest single drop in the eastern United States. The falls are off U.S. 64 on an unpaved road near Oakland, between Cashiers and Lake Toxaway.

HIGH HAMPTON INN AND COUNTRY CLUB

Route 107, Cashiers, North Carolina. Mailing address: P.O. Box 338, Cashiers, NC 28717. 704-743-2411. *Innkeeper:* William D. McKee. Open April 1 to November 1.

High Hampton Inn, ringed by the Appalachian Mountains, is on 2,600 acres of woodland. Its extensive resort–country club offerings include horse and foot trails, a golf course designed by George W. Cobb, excellent tennis facilities, a man-made lake for swimming, trout fishing, and quiet boating, and a fine stable of horses. At this peaceful mountain retreat, guests can slip away alone to the high mountain trails or join in the many well-planned and organized activities, such as trap and skeet shooting, mountain arts and crafts, and square dancing and mountain clogging. The prime mover of this estate is the inn's owner and gracious host, Bill McKee.

High Hampton has a long history as a summer retreat. It began in the early nineteenth century as the summer home of the Hampton family, South Carolina plantation aristocracy. Wade Hampton III, a general in Lee's army and then a governor and U.S. Senator from South Carolina, summered here. The property was then passed on to the general's niece and her husband, Dr. Halsted, who were respon-sible for the beautifully landscaped grounds. The doctor bought up the surrounding farms to increase his landholdings; one such pur-chase led to the haunting of High Hampton. A neighboring farmer's wife swore she would die if her home was sold, and when her husband returned home from selling the land to Dr. Halsted, he found her hanging from an oak tree. According to local legend, a snowy white owl flew screeching about the dead woman's head as she hung there. To this day they say that the owls heard frequently at night here are the farmer's wife crying over the loss of the land.

Both Dr. Halsted and his wife died in 1922; High Hampton was purchased by Bill McKee's father, and began its life as an inn. The entire place burned to the ground in a fire in 1932. The present inn was built in 1933 in a rough mountain style, with handcrafted rustic furniture fashioned by local Appalachian-mountain craftspeople. The lodge is constructed of large timbers and covered with chestnut bark shingles, giving it the appearance of a much older building. The grounds around the resort have sheer granite cliffs and green mountains reflecting in the lake's crystal-clear waters. There are 130 rooms in the inn and the many secluded cottages on the estate. The cottages have shady porches, and many have the same rough chestnut siding as the lodge itself. They contain three or four guest rooms furnished with handcrafted wooden pieces and colorful hooked rugs. Each cottage's sitting room is shared by occupants of its guest rooms. There are comfortable chairs and couches and fireplaces with ample supplies of wood. The guest rooms in the inn consist of rough pine-paneling with wooden furniture and simple mountain décor. Many of these rooms also have their own fireplaces.

The inn's spacious lounge features a four-sided stone fireplace with fires in each of its hearths in cool weather. In addition to the handcrafted furnishings there are many overstuffed chairs and couches and plenty of game tables set up for guests' enjoyment in the dark-paneled room. The lower level includes a gift shop and sports-supply store.

The dining room serves hearty buffet-style meals featuring the inn's smoke-cured hams from their own smokehouse. The vegetables come fresh from the inn's gardens, and all the breads and pastries come warm from the ovens to the table. Bill McKee shares his love of fine food with his guests. Meals range from mountain fare to French haute cuisine to Southern-style cooking. There are mountain-trout dishes, a shad roe supreme, souffléed asparagus, and more. Alcoholic beverages are not served, but setups are available for guests who wish to bring their own. All three daily meals are open to guests and the public.

Accommodations: 130 rooms with private bath. *Pets:* Permitted, but must be kept in the inn's kennels (free). *Driving Instructions:* The inn is 2 miles south of Cashiers on Route 107.

Charlotte, North Carolina

HAMPTON MANOR

3327 Carmel Road, Charlotte, NC 28226. 704-542-6299. *Innkeeper:* Rebecca W. Triggs. Open all year.

If one wants to be pampered, the Hampton Manor will oblige. A Rolls Royce Silver Shadow picks guests up at the airport and whisks them off to an English-style manor house filled with museum-quality antiques and an attentive, uniformed staff. The manor sits on the site of a large plantation house. The creation of the present Hampton Manor was inspired by Rosehill, an 1840s mansion in Yorkshire, England. It doesn't seem possible today to find craftsmen who can create richly paneled walls and lavish high-ceilinged rooms with ornate plasterwork, but Hampton Manor is proof to the contrary. The furnishings are all formal European antiques. The Churchill Room has English pieces, while the Louis XV Room is lavishly French. The Great Chamber Suite features a large sixteenth-century Elizabethan bed and medieval trappings to which a hot-tub has been added. Afternoon teas are served in the English pub downstairs. A full English breakfast is served in the guest rooms. Although no other meals are served, the chauffeur-driven Rolls takes guests to and from dinner.

Accommodations: 4 rooms with private bath. *Pets:* Not permitted. *Driving Instructions:* The inn is on Carmel Road in Charlotte.

Chimney Rock, North Carolina

CORBETT HOUSE BED AND BREAKFAST

Box 134, Route 74, Chimney Rock, NC 28720. 704-625-4403. *Innkeepers:* Anne and Bob Corbett. Open all year.

Chimney Rock is a quaint little town lined with mountain craft shops and restaurants, along the banks of the Rocky Broad River in the shadow of Chimney Rock Park. Nearby, Hickory Nut Falls, one of the highest waterfalls in the eastern United States, drops 404 feet down a sheer granite cliff. At one end of the town, beside an old bridge, stands Corbett House, where Chimney Rock looms high above, the sound of the tumbling river fills the mountain air, and the lawn stretches down to the riverbank.

The inn is most inviting with its creamy-yellow clapboard trimmed in soft blues. Rockers and hanging baskets of flowers on the decks and porches overlooking the river and mountains add to the charm. Inside, a spacious living room, with its spinning wheel, buggy seat, and grouping of comfortable couches and chairs, shares space with the innkeepers' folk-art shop, which offers antiques, quilts, and handmade items. The cream-colored walls and staircase are hand-stenciled in blue, while the guest rooms are furnished with country-pine pieces and handmade quilts. Breakfast is served on the porch in nice weather.

Accommodations: 7 rooms with shared baths. *Pets:* Not permitted. *Driving Instructions:* The inn is 18 miles southeast of Asheville and 17 miles east of Hendersonville.

ESMERALDA INN

U.S. Highway 74, Chimney Rock, North Carolina. Mailing address: Box 57, Chimney Rock, NC 28720. 704-625-9105. *Innkeepers:* Pete and Pam Smith. Open April through mid-November.

The Esmeralda Inn is on a hillside overlooking the mountains and Rocky Broad River across the road. Two stories of screened verandas span the rustic mountain retreat, built at the turn of the century and once a popular location for silent films. It was the hideout of a number of movie stars, including Clark Gable, Mary Pickford, and Douglas Fairbanks in their heyday. For lovers of the rustic country look, one step into the lobby and you know you are home. The peeled-log room features a wraparound balcony of logs held up by massive timbers, a big stone hearth, and stuffed owls and hawks perched on supports. A mounted deer head adorns one wall, and bearskins and trophies decorate others. Bedrooms, which open onto verandas or the balcony, are simply furnished, with antique quilts for color, carpeted floors, and painted board-and-batten walls, although a few rooms have modern paneling. The dining room, with a screened porch that is glassed-in for cold weather, is open to the public for lunch on Sunday and dinner Tuesday through Saturday. A Continental breakfast is served to guests in the lobby.

Accommodations: 13 rooms, 7 with private bath. *Pets:* Not permitted. *Driving Instructions:* The inn is on Route 74, 22 miles east of Asheville.

Clemmons, North Carolina

Clemmons is the home of *Tanglewood Park* with full recreational activities open to the public. Tanglewood is 10 miles west of Winston-Salem, with its variety of historic and cultural offerings. *Old Salem,* in the heart of the city, is a restored Moravian Congregational town of the late eighteenth century and early nineteenth century. Many of the restored homes and buildings are open to the public for a nominal fee. The *Museum of Early Southern Decorative Arts (MESDA)* has many period rooms exhibiting the arts of the South from the 1600s to 1820. Green directional markers lead to the historic area and the *Old Salem Reception Center,* where the tours begin. *Reynolds House* offers an outstanding collection of American art displayed in the former home of R. J. Reynolds, founder of the Reynolds Tobacco Company. Tours of the *R. J. Reynolds Tobacco Company* and the *Joseph Schlitz Brewing Company* are offered to the public all year.

TANGLEWOOD MANOR HOUSE, LODGE, AND RESTAURANT

Tanglewood Park, Clemmons, North Carolina. Mailing address: P.O. Box 1040, Clemmons, NC 27012. 919-766-0591. *Innkeeper:* Mrs. Brenda Sanders. Open all year.

The Manor House at Tanglewood Park is the centerpiece of the 1,117-acre estate of the late Mr. and Mrs. William N. Reynolds. The park was deeded to Forsyth County by the Reynoldses, who wished to share Tanglewood's beauty. The estate was aptly described by the late Bishop Douglas L. Rights: "With the Yadkin River flowing nearby, the productive fields and orchards, flowerbeds, the ancient trees near the house and the woodland beyond, the stables and Mr. Will's racetrack, here was a delightful homeplace." The park is now a large, complete public recreation resort with rustic woodland cabins, a motel-lodge with patios and balconies overlooking wooded glens, and the Manor House itself, all offering overnight guest facilities. The Manor House was built in 1859 with several later additions and was completely renovated near the turn of the century. The house has rather formally furnished guest rooms with matching spreads and drapes of soft floral patterns complementing the pastel satins and velvets of the upholstered love seats and chairs. Several rooms have the original fireplaces, and all have views of the flowering trees.

The estate features many year-round recreational opportunities. The park provides the breeding and training of quarter horses, thoroughbreds, and show horses at the stable facilities in addition to trail riding and lessons. There is even a racetrack where the Tanglewood Steeplechase is held each May. There are also excellent tennis facilities and two eighteen-hole championship golf courses including one designed by Robert Trent Jones that was the site of a past PGA national championship. Paddleboats and canoes can be rented at Mallard Lake. Tanglewood also has a deer park, gardens, a nineteenth-century church and graveyard, and a parked train-engine to climb aboard. The park is a beautiful recreation and overnight facility in the rolling countryside just west of Winston-Salem.

Accommodations: 11 rooms in the Manor House, all with private bath, plus 18 motel units and 7 cottages. *Pets:* Not permitted in the park or overnight facilities by state law. Kennels available nearby. *Driving Instructions:* Take I-40 west of Winston-Salem about 10 miles to the Tanglewood exit.

Dillsboro, North Carolina

THE JARRETT HOUSE

P.O. Box 219, Dillsboro, NC 28725. 704-586-9964. *Innkeepers:* Jim and Jean Hartbarger. Open Easter through October.

When the railroad came to Dillsboro in 1880, the town's founder, William Allen Dills, saw a chance to capitalize on the increasing transient population it would bring. Two years later he built a hotel he called the Mount Beulah Hotel after his youngest daughter. Over the years, many a passenger would disembark just before noon to enjoy a dinner for which reservations had been telegraphed ahead by the railroad company. In 1894, Dills sold his thriving business to R. Frank Jarrett, who renamed the hotel the Jarrett Springs Hotel to call attention to sulfur springs he had discovered in the rear of the property. After indulging in the good country cooking, visitors could now sit by the spring and sip the odorous but reputedly invigorating waters. Jarrett cured his own hams and served so much food that he offered to give a free meal to anyone asking for a refill of the meat plate. As far as is known, he never had to make good on the offer.

The traditions continue today at the Jarrett House, and heading the list are the heaping plates of food featuring country ham and red-eye gravy, fried chicken, or mountain trout, accompanied by country treats like candied apples, pickled beets, coleslaw, fresh vegetables, vinegar pie, and fresh-baked cobblers. Many a belt has been loosened after a meal at the Jarrett House.

The inn is a restoration that was a labor of love for the Hartbargers, involving the stripping of all the paint off the original furniture throughout the inn to reveal the auburn tones of turn-of-the-century oak. The guest rooms are delightfully old-fashioned, with sheer curtains, rockers, and period beds and chests. The inn's exterior has three-tiered porches festooned with wrought-iron railings and column decorations. On the porch are rockers that serve guests today as they did seventy-five years ago.

Accommodations: 19 rooms with private bath. *Pets:* Not permitted. *Children:* Under twelve not permitted. *Driving Instructions:* Dillsboro is 47 miles west of Asheville, and the inn is at the intersection of Routes 23-19A and 19A-441.

SQUIRE WATKINS INN

Haywood Road, Dillsboro, North Carolina. Mailing address: P.O. Box 430, Dillsboro, NC 28725. 704-586-5244. *Innkeepers:* Tom and Emma Wertenberger. Open all year.

Flora and J.C. Watkins were among the first settlers of Dillsboro, where they built their large family home in the 1800s on a hillside at the edge of town. The house remained in the Watkins family until 1983 when Tom and Emma Wertenberger bought it, fulfilling a dream of becoming country "innkeepers."

Although the house was badly in need of care—it remained mercifully unscathed by "modernization"—the Wertenbergers have done a good job of restoring their country-Victorian and nearby carriage house, which now contains an antique and mountain-craft shop. The inn's high-ceilinged rooms are decorated with Victorian antiques, with several comfortable modern pieces in the parlor. Two guest rooms have big kitty-corner bay windows, one has its own separate sitting room and fireplace, and all have fresh flowers and turn-down service for guests. A Continental breakfast is served to guests only in the formal dining room or in the more casual solarium. Three housekeeping cottages have working fireplaces as well. The inn is surrounded by three acres of terraced gardens. Steep stone stairs lead to the railroad tracks, where in the years of whistle-stops, one could flag down a passing train, though now just one or two roll by daily.

Accommodations: 5 rooms, 2 with private bath, and 3 cottages. *Pets and children under 12:* Not permitted. *Driving Instructions:* Take Route 23/19A or 23/441 to Dillsboro. The inn is at the intersection.

Edenton, North Carolina

THE LORDS PROPRIETORS' INN

300 North Broad Street, Edenton, NC 27932. 919-482-3641. *Innkeepers:* Arch and Jane F. Edwards. Open all year except Christmas.

In 1663, Charles II granted the land of North Carolina to eight Lords Proprietors and their successors. The inn named in their honor comprises three adjacent historic homes, two Victorian and the other built in 1790 and remodeled at the turn of the twentieth century. The restored buildings retain many of their original ornamental trappings, such as stained-glass windows, carved-oak railings, and lacy, painted-oak fretwork in the entry hall. The rooms are decorated with coordinated colors and fabrics that complement the many European and American antiques. The Edwardses invited local antique dealers and collectors to furnish the rooms around themes representing a particular period. The results are a success down to the smallest details—the prints on the walls, the quilts and antique bedcovers, and even the pillow shams. The guest room beds, many of them graceful pencil-posters, are locally crafted. Arrangements may be made to purchase these as well as antiques used and displayed at the inn.

Guests are served a Continental breakfast of breads, rolls, and muffins baked by the innkeeper and accompanied by pots of home-made preserves and fruits. Edenton, a little Southern town on the spit of land between Albemarle Sound and the Chowan River, served for several years as the Colonial capital of North Carolina, and a number of its historic buildings remain. Guided tours are available.

Accommodations: 18 rooms with private bath. *Pets:* Not permitted. *Driving Instructions:* Edenton is on Route 17, between Norfolk, Virginia, and New Bern, North Carolina.

Flat Rock, North Carolina

WOODFIELD INN

Highway 25, Flat Rock, North Carolina. Mailing address: P.O. Box 98, Flat Rock, NC 28731. 704-693-6016. *Innkeeper:* David Levin. Open all year.

The Woodfield Inn, which claims to be North Carolina's oldest operating inn, was built between 1850 and 1852 and has never closed, except during a thorough restoration several years ago. Under the guidance of several experts on Victorian decor, the old inn has been transformed into a splendid period inn with large bedrooms, salons, and halls typical of the era. The living room is decorated with camelback sofas and loveseats, a large crystal chandelier, Oriental carpets, ornate gilded mirrors, and antique tapestries and samplers. The entry hall and staircase walls are papered with boldly patterned prints. A large carved trunk — large enough to entomb an elephant — is set against one wall. The guest rooms and suites, some with working fireplaces, are furnished with Victorian oak furniture, decorative quilts, lace curtains, and ceiling fans. One room still has the secret opening in its floor where soldiers were hidden during the Civil War.

The dining room and sun porch are open to the guests and public for meals, where dinner entrées include steaks, chicken, ribs, roast duckling, South Carolina flounder, and mountain trout. Two stories of latticed verandas with wicker porch furniture offer views of the sweeping lawn, tall pines, statuary, and a latticed dance pavilion.

Accommodations: 27 rooms and suites, all with private bath. *Pets:* By prior arrangement only. *Driving Instructions:* The inn is on Route 25, about 2½ miles south of Hendersonville.

Franklin, North Carolina

THE FRANKLIN TERRACE

67 Harrison Avenue, Franklin, NC 28734. 704-524-7907. *Innkeepers:* Mike and Pat Giampola. Open May through October.

The twenty-room, two-story inn has high ceilings, tall windows, and wide covered porches on both the first and second floors. Guest rooms are furnished with antiques, and most have lovely views of the Smoky Mountains. The decor is turn of the century, and the atmosphere is casual. All rooms have private bath and television.

The Franklin Terrace was built in 1887 as the Academy of Learning, a semiprivate academy for girls. Since completion of its restoration, the inn has been listed in the National Register of Historic Places.

The first floor of The Franklin Terrace houses an old-fashioned sweet shop and several antique shops. Open from 2 to 10 P.M., the sweet shop serves an assortment of pies and cheesecakes as well as ice cream sodas, sundaes, shakes, and banana splits.

The inn is near the Cowee Valley Ruby Mines. Visitors may try their hand at mining the gems.

Accommodations: 7 rooms and 1 cottage, all with private bath. *Pets:* Not permitted. *Children:* Under 12 not permitted. *Driving Instructions:* Franklin may be reached by Route 441 from the north or south or by Route 64 from the east or west.

POOR RICHARD'S SUMMIT INN

East Rogers Street, Franklin, North Carolina. Mailing address: P.O. Box 511, Franklin, NC 28734. 704-524-2006. *Innkeepers:* Lloyd Woosley, Jr., and Minnie Hays. Open all year.

In 1898, S. L. Rogers, a prominent Franklin resident, constructed this wood-shingled, many-gabled home on a hill overlooking what was then a sleepy pastoral hamlet. Twenty years later the home was converted into an inn to serve the many travelers who were drawn to the nearby Smoky and Blue Ridge mountains. In the half century since, the town at the foot of the inn's hilltop has grown rapidly and has swallowed up the farmland. However, the Summit Inn remains a sanctuary and a monument to the simpler life of another era.

Within its walls, the innkeepers have preserved the feeling of a turn-of-the-century inn with spacious guest rooms filled with iron, brass, or Victorian high-back beds, crocheted spreads, braided rag or Oriental rugs on the floors, marble fireplace mantels, and paddle fans on most ceilings. Each room has a collection of antique decorative pieces.

Much of the inn's first floor is devoted to its many dining rooms, ranging in size from intimate rooms seating four to six to the main room with myriad potted and hanging plants, lace tablecloths, and floral centerpieces.

A number of the dining rooms have their own fireplaces. In one, a wood-fired cookstove keeps the soup pot bubbling. (In fact, the fireplaces and wood stoves supply the heat at the Summit during the winter months, augmented in the guest rooms by electric blankets.) Dining at the Summit is about evenly divided between seafood dishes such as lobster in a skillet, sautéed scallops, fresh mountain trout, and shrimp tempura, and Continental dishes such as baked chicken curry, broiled lamb chops, filet mignon, and roast Long Island duckling. A house specialty is hickory-smoked country ham with red-eye gravy. Certainly a best buy is Poor Richard's All You Can Eat dinners featuring an assortment of meats, soup, salads, vegetables, and wild rice.

Many of the inn's oak pieces are in its living room, where a large Oriental rug rich in reds accents the red of a large Victorian couch. The fireplace in the alcove is built of native stones. This room also contains the inn's only television set. Franklin is called by many the "Gem Capital of the Country," and in the evening you can often hear guests swapping stories of their finds in the many ruby and sapphire mines open to the public in the surrounding hills. Although you aren't likely to get rich at one of these mines, they do provide entertainment for all members of the family.

Accommodations: 15 rooms, 7 with private bath. *Pets:* Not permitted. *Driving Instructions:* From Route 441, take Business Route 441 to East Rogers Street. The inn is at the top of the hill.

REVERIE

1197 Greenville Highway, Hendersonville, NC 28739. 704-693-8255. *Innkeepers:* Michael Abriola and Kathy Price. Open all year, except January and February.

Reverie was built as a boarding house in 1911, so it is not surprising to discover that it is particularly well laid out as a bed-and-breakfast inn. When Kathy and Michael discovered the house, they fell in love with it. They were already in love with each other and exchanged wedding vows in the inn's sun room just two months before Reverie opened to the public. Michael is a computer-consultant-turned-innkeeper, and Kathy is an emergency room physician in neighboring Brevard.

The innkeepers have decorated Reverie's interior in hues of rose, violet, and blue. The living room is furnished with Victorian pieces, and each bedroom has pieces dating from the Victorian through Art Deco periods. A Continental breakfast is served in the dining room or sun room at either a formal mahogany pedestal table or at two small white-wicker dining settings. The inn, in the heart of the Blue Ridge Mountains, stands on about an acre of land, which the innkeepers are busy filling with plantings, including roses, azaleas, and rhododendrons, as well as a profusion of iris and tulips. Nearby, the stately Biltmore House, now open to the public as a museum, was constructed by George Vanderbilt and is a reminder of turn-of-the-century elegance when the wealthy of Charleston and New York spent their summers in the area.

Accommodations: 8 rooms, 2 with private bath. *Pets:* Not permitted. *Children:* Under 12 not permitted. *Smoking:* Not permitted. *Driving Instructions:* Reverie is one mile south of Hendersonville on Route 25.

Highlands, North Carolina

THE OLD EDWARDS INN

Main Street, Highlands, North Carolina. *Mailing address:* Box 1778, Highlands, NC 28741. 704-526-5036. *Innkeepers:* Pat and Rip Benton. Open May through October.

In the mountaintop town of Highlands is the Old Edwards Inn, an imposing three-story hostelry. It consists of the original wood-framed building that was completed in 1883 and a larger brick structure built in the 1930s.

Innkeepers Rip and Pat Benton, who had been searching for an old inn in need of restoration and loving care, discovered this inn, which had stood empty for eighteen years when they first saw it. They gathered up the many antiques they had collected over the years for their antique shop and restaurant in Saint Simons Island and installed them in the inn's carefully restored rooms. New wallpapers were matched as closely as possible to the faded originals still on the walls. Master stenciler Brenda Kellum applied whimsical Victorian designs to the halls and guest rooms, using animal, pineapple, and bird motifs. The guest rooms, many with balconies, have iron or brass beds or wooden Victorian sets with patchwork quilts.

Accommodations: 21 rooms with private bath. *Pets:* Not permitted. *Driving Instructions:* To reach Highlands, take Route 28 from the north or south or Route 64 from the east.

MILL HOUSE BED & BREAKFAST

Route 64, Highlands, NC 28741. 704-526-3140 or 704-526-2936.
Innkeeper: Elizabeth Clarkson. Open May through October.

Mill House is perched precariously on rocky ledges at the edge of a waterfall. A large waterwheel and sluiceway at one time supplied electricity, but now is only ornamental. Innkeeper Libby Clarkson's father, a civil engineer, built Mill House as a family retreat on the site of an old mill some fifty years ago.

Today, the bed-and-breakfast inn looks like a fantasy cottage out of a fairy tale, rustic and quaint with a big stone fireplace, red painted wood floors topped with colorful rag rugs and, throughout, the sound of the water. Inside, the inn's walls are board and batten, and each guest bedroom is unique. One, Treetops Room, has a view of the waterfall from its bed. Another, which has its own balcony overlooking the falls, is said to have its own rather pleasant ghost, although she rarely makes appearances these days. Guests are welcome to fix their own meals and to use the canoe for a paddle on the lake above the falls.

Accommodations: 6 rooms with shared baths. *Pets:* Not permitted. *Driving Instructions:* The inn is one mile from the center of Highlands, on Route 64.

Hillsborough, North Carolina

Off I-85 between Greensboro and Durham is the historic town of Hillsborough. Founded in 1754, it was the state capital for a short time during the Revolution. The Greek Revival Orange County Courthouse contains an unbroken sequence of wills and deeds from 1756 and has a cupola with a clock said to have been donated to the town by George III. The *Orange County Historical Museum* is located in the second-floor courtroom of the courthouse, and its collection includes a brass-and-copper set of weights and measures acquired in 1790 and, in its Homespun Room, several old looms. The town has many historic buildings, which may be seen on a walking tour that has been outlined by the historical society. Pick up a pamphlet at the museum or write them at 110 East Orange Street, Hillsborough, NC 27278.

COLONIAL INN

153 West King Street, Hillsborough, NC 27278. 919-732-2461. *Innkeepers:* Carolyn B. Welsh and Evelyn B. Atkins. Open all year except Christmas week.

A tavern has stood on the spot now occupied by the Colonial Inn since

1759, although the oldest part of the current structure dates back to 1768, having been constructed when the original tavern burned. The white-clapboard inn with its long veranda and upstairs balcony has a rich history in a town that has seen more than its share of important events. Lord Cornwallis, who made his headquarters at the inn in 1781, was so annoyed with the muddy streets that he had his men lay flat flagstones in front of the hotel and out in several directions. Aaron Burr was a guest at the inn before his vice-presidency.

The inn was very nearly destroyed when General Sherman's "Bummers" raided Hillsborough in 1865, ransacking and pillaging anything of value. The innkeeper's widow, Sarah Stroud, saved the day by waving her husband's Masonic apron to the soldiers below, and a Masonic sergeant who spotted the emblem demanded that his soldiers return the spoils to the inn and guard it to prevent further pillage.

Today, the Colonial Inn offers small and comfortable guest rooms in the restored building, as well as public dining for lunch and dinner. Breakfast is served to guests only. The inn's public rooms include four dining rooms, some with bare wooden tables, wagon-wheel lamps, and shuttered windows, others with white linen service and exposed beams. Several have fireplaces, and all feature Southern cooking, with offerings that include Southern pan-fried chicken, Brunswick stew, chicken and dumplings, fried okra, tomato pudding, and the always popular North Carolina country-cured ham dinner. Many antiques are found throughout the inn. The lobby with its fireplace watched over by an ancestral painting has an old spinning wheel, deacon's bench, cane-backed rocker, and cobbler's bench. The inn has polished hardwood and wide-plank floors with area rugs in some parts along with upholstered sofas of more recent vintage.

Accommodations: 12 rooms, 8 with private bath. *Pets:* Not permitted. *Driving Instructions:* Take exit 164 from Route 85 between Greensboro and Durham; proceed ½ mile to Hillsborough and turn left at the King Street traffic light. The inn is one block on the left.

Linville, North Carolina

Just off the Blue Ridge Parkway in western North Carolina, Linville
is best known as the site of *Grandfather Mountain,* one of the highest
(5,964 feet) in the Blue Ridge range. A privately owned toll road leads
to the *Mile High Swinging Bridge* that connects two peaks (access off
Route 221). There are hiking trails, a visitor's center, and a museum of
natural history. The site is open from April to November; admission
is charged. Call 704-733-4337. Annual events include *Singing on the
Mountain* in late June and *Grandfather Mountain Highland Games*
(traditional Scottish games by more than one hundred clans) in early
July. *Linville Caverns* offers a tour of the stalagmites and stalactites
along a lighted underground river.

ESEEOLA LODGE

Routes 221, 181, and 105, Linville, North Carolina. Mailing ad-
dress: P.O. Box 98, Linville, NC 28646. 704-733-4311. *Innkeeper:*
John M. Blackburn. Open from June 1 through Labor Day.
There has been a summer lodge at this location since 1892, when an

elaborate Victorian structure was built to serve the needs of summer vacationers. The original building was destroyed by fire, and the current building was erected in two stages in 1926 and 1936. Eseeola Lodge is distinguished by chestnut-bark siding and the peeled-chestnut and poplar poles that support the numerous gabled porches. With Grandfather Mountain as a backdrop and Kawana Lake just a mile away, the lodge offers guest rooms in a resort setting that includes an eighteen-hole Donald Ross golf course, eight all-weather tennis courts, a heated swimming pool, horseback riding, and an organized recreational program for children.

Most of the furnishings in the twenty-eight chestnut-paneled guest rooms were made by a woodworking shop set up by the original owners for the purpose. The beds, dressers, night stands, and other furniture are of the same chestnut as the building. The lodge was completely refurbished in 1982.

The lodge has a large lounge and a smaller lobby, both with native stone fireplaces, a card room, and a television room. There is no television in the guest rooms. The dining room serves two meals a day, with the public invited to all on an advance-reservation basis. Each day the selections at dinner change. Typical of the entrées prepared by Eseeola's Swiss chef are poached salmon, roast prime ribs, roast filet mignon, blanquette de veau, and numerous poultry and steak preparations.

Accommodations: 28 guest rooms. *Pets:* Not permitted. *Driving Instructions:* The lodge is a mile off the Blue Ridge Parkway in the center of Linville.

New Bern, North Carolina

KINGS ARMS

212 Pollock Street. New Bern, North Carolina. Mailing address: Box 1085, New Bern, NC 28560. 919-638-4409. Open all year.

Most visitors to New Bern come to tour Tryon Palace, the superbly restored governor's residence of the Royal Colony of North Carolina. Furnished with eighteenth- and nineteenth-century English and American antiques, the Palace was a center of activities leading to the American Revolution. However, the entire town is filled with handsome residences, many dating from the post-Revolutionary Federal period. It was in response to the need to provide overnight housing for tourists who appreciated early architecture that the idea of opening the Kings Arms arose.

Three couples bought the old Pollock Street house and began a detailed restoration of the three-story structure that was to become their inn. The house itself is an interesting example of emerging American architecture. The front portion was probably built about 1847, with additions continuing until the early 1900s. A mansard roof was added then that converted its look to the Victorian period, although the front of the building remains clearly a part of the mid-nineteenth century. Inside the house, the innkeepers have created guest rooms that have modern features like wall-to-wall carpeting, air conditioning, and modern baths but that retain the original woodwork, hearths, and other architectural features of its period. Canopied, poster, and brass beds are the rule, and the decor is more of the colonial and Federal periods than of the Victorian era.

Accommodations: 11 rooms, 8 with private bath. *Pets:* Not permitted. *Driving Instructions:* Take Route 17 across the Neuse River Bridge, turn left on East Front Street, go one block, and turn right on Pollock Street.

Pinehurst, North Carolina

THE MAGNOLIA INN

Magnolia Road, Pinehurst, North Carolina. *Mailing address:* Box 266, Pinehurst, NC 28374. 919-295-6900. *Innkeeper:* Leslie Wilson. Open all year.

The Magnolia Inn was built in 1896 by the Tufts family of Boston. A half-century earlier Pinehurst had been founded by James Tufts, and it operated as a private village and resort until 1971. Pinehurst continues to be preeminent as a winter resort known best for its six golf courses at the Pinehurst Country Club, where the inn has guest privileges.

The Magnolia is an imposing three-story building with a mansard-style roof pierced by many dormers. Porches are everywhere at The Magnolia, including twin porches at opposite ends of its second floor. Each porch and the guest rooms overlook the hotel's grounds and their magnolia and holly trees as well as camellias and azaleas.

The inn's twin-bedded guest rooms are air-conditioned. The living room has a large fireplace, and guests often gather here to watch television. The dining room, where breakfast is served, is bright and cheerful. The Magnolia's location facing the main street of this historic village makes it possible for guests to leave their cars parked at the hotel and walk to nearby shops and restaurants.

Accommodations: 12 rooms with private bath. *Pets:* Not permitted. *Driving Instructions:* Pinehurst is reached from the north or south by Route 15-501.

Pollocksville, North Carolina

TRENT RIVER PLANTATION

U.S. 17, Pollocksville, North Carolina. Mailing address: P.O. Box 154, Pollocksville, NC 28573. 919-224-3811. *Innkeepers:* Bill Parker and John K. Williams. Open March through Thanksgiving.

Trent River Plantation is an old estate, now open to overnight guests, on landscaped grounds beside the picturesque Trent River. The grounds are shaded by large pines, magnolias, live oaks, and pecan trees. Flowers bloom in profusion almost all year: In winter there are camellias, and in spring azaleas and dogwoods are everywhere. In summer a large heated swimming pool is also decorated with flowers.

The manor house, built in the late nineteenth century, contains

antiques from the late eighteenth and early nineteenth centuries. The guest rooms are elegantly appointed with formal antiques, and three of the five rooms have four-poster canopied beds. A decanter of sherry is set out on the marble-topped bureau as a welcoming touch for overnight guests, who are served breakfast and given private tours of the grounds and farm. A personal guide is available for fishing expeditions on the river.

Accommodations: 5 rooms with shared baths. *Driving Instructions:* The plantation is on U.S. 17, 10 miles southwest of New Bern.

THE OAKWOOD INN

411 North Bloodworth Street, Raleigh, NC 27604. 919-832-9712. *Innkeepers:* Deborah Lamm. Open all year.

The Oakwood Inn is named for Historic Oakwood, a twenty-square-block district encompassing many Victorian homes. Typical of the neighborhood is the Oakwood Inn, an 1871 house now listed in the National Register of Historic Places. True to the period, Victorian colors and papers are used throughout, and in all, there are nine fireplaces. A comfortable parlor is available to guests, as is the formal dining room where full Southern breakfasts are served. Only period antiques — no reproductions — have been used at the inn. Printed walking tour guides are available for guests who wish to explore Historic Oakwood. Parking is available at the rear of the inn.

Accommodations: 6 guest rooms, 2 with private bath. *Pets and children under 12:* Not permitted. *Driving Instructions:* Route I-40 becomes Wade Avenue in Raleigh. Take Wade to Glenwood and turn Right. Drive to P Street (the first stoplight) and turn left. Take P Street to Blunt and turn right on Polk Street. Take Polk 2 blocks to Bloodworth.

Robbinsville, North Carolina

BLUE BOAR LODGE

Route 1, Robbinsville, NC 28771. 704-479-8126. *Innkeepers:* Roy and Kathy Wilson. Open April to October and for hunting only from mid-October to January.

Blue Boar Lodge, a secluded mountain retreat in a hollow in the foothills of the Smokies, is the perfect hideaway. It is surrounded by Nantahala National Forest and the beautiful Joyce Kilmer Memorial Forest. An old plank bridge leads across a mountain stream to forest trails. The lodge's front porch overlooks the trout pond with its resident wild ducks. One can observe the comings and goings of the many varieties of birds here including tiny hummingbirds and colorful cardinals. Only the sounds of the mountain breezes and the mountain stream disturb the quiet.

The living room is an inviting place to relax after a day of hiking and fishing. The big stone fireplace has stuffed trophy heads that enhance the rustic mountain atmosphere. There is a game room equipped for billiards, darts, and table tennis.

Guests gather for all meals around the lazy-Susan table where everything is served family style and all can eat to their heart's content. Just about everything that is offered is prepared from scratch: fish from the stocked pond, fresh vegetables from the lodge garden, homemade pickles, jellies, breads, and pastries.

A mile from the Blue Boar is Lake Santeetlah, a mountain lake with 108 miles of secluded shoreline. Swimming, boating, fishing, and canoeing are excellent. Boats and canoes can be rented, and bait is available.

Accommodations: 8 rooms with private bath. *Pets:* Not permitted May to October. *Driving Instructions:* The lodge is two hours south of Knoxville, Tennessee, via Route 129, or two hours west of Asheville, North Carolina, via routes 129 and 19. It is on Joyce Kilmer Forest Road.

SNOWBIRD MOUNTAIN LODGE

Joyce Kilmer Forest Road, Robbinsville, North Carolina. Mailing address: RD1. Box 49A, Robbinsville, NC 28771. 704-479-3433. *Innkeepers:* Bob and Connie Rhudy. Open May through early November.

Built in 1941, Snowbird Mountain Lodge is perched on the mountainside at an elevation of 2,880 feet. Constructed of chestnut logs and stone, it is small enough to be intimate (a maximum of thirty-six guests), yet large enough to have a complete dining room and to offer a variety of recreational activities. Each of the wood-paneled guest rooms is furnished with sturdy wooden beds and other simple furnishings. Two stone fireplaces are frequently fired up to dispel the chill of the evening mountain air. The main lounge has a cathedral ceiling with hand-hewn solid-chestnut beams. This room is paneled in butternut. The dining room, paneled in wild cherry, serves meals such as trout amandine, New York strip steak, and prime ribs of beef. The Rhudys take pride in their home-baked rolls, cakes, and pies.

There are miles of hiking trails through the Joyce Kilmer Memorial Forest, where guests can discover old Indian paths or, if more adventurous, climb to the nearby peaks. The lodge has shuffleboard, table tennis, croquet, horseshoes, badminton, miniature bowling, and skittles. There is swimming in a natural spring-fed pool of the local mountain stream, and fishing and canoeing in the streams and nearby lakes. White-water rafting is popular on the Nantahala River nearby.

Accommodations: 22 rooms with private bath. *Pets:* Not permitted. *Children:* Under twelve not permitted. *Driving Instructions:* Take Route 19 to Topton, then follow Route 129 to Robbinsville. Follow the signs to the forest and the lodge.

Saluda, North Carolina

THE ORCHARD INN

Highway 176, Saluda, North Carolina. Mailing address: P.O. Box 725, Saluda, NC 28773. 704-749-5471. *Innkeepers:* Ann and Ken Hough. Open all year.

The Orchard Inn is on a hillside at an elevation of 2500 feet. Its secluded 18 acres are at the end of a winding mountain drive through woodlands criss-crossed with walking paths. From the clearing behind the inn, one can enjoy vistas of the Warrior Mountain Range. In warm weather, flowers line the walk leading to the inn, and pots of hanging geraniums add color to the porch and its rustic rockers. Ken and Ann Hough have transformed their turn-of-the-century mountain retreat into an inn filled with family antiques, hand-crafted quilts, rag rugs, and decorative mountain crafts. The living room, with a fieldstone fireplace and large airtight stove, is more formal, with potted palms and groupings of wing chairs and loveseats on Oriental carpets. Bowls of potpouri, dried floral wreaths, ruffled throw pillows, and antique silver add appealing touches. A well-stocked library is tucked in an alcove, and a craft shop is housed on a porch.

The guest rooms, each with a private bath, are fancifully decorated with tiny floral print wallpapers, puffs on antique beds, and stenciled apples in some rooms. The glassed-in dining room, with its mountain views, serves breakfast to house guests and lunches and dinners to the public by reservation. Lunch is served daily except Saturday, and dinners, all but Sunday night. The inn is in a dry county, but guests can purchase alcoholic beverages in nearby towns.

Accommodations: 11 rooms with private bath. *Pets and children under 6:* Not permitted. *Driving Instructions:* The inn is on Route 176 midway between Hendersonville and Tryon.

Tryon, North Carolina

MILL FARM INN

Route 108, Tryon, North Carolina. Mailing address: P.O. Box 1251, Tryon, NC 28782. 704-859-6992. *Innkeepers:* Chip and Penny Kessler. Open March through November.

Mill Farm Inn, on 3½ acres of landscaped grounds stretching down to the Pacolet River, is a handsome stone building constructed in 1939. Inside, guests find rooms with contemporary furniture and wall-to-wall shag carpeting. The common room has exposed chestnut beams and a stone fireplace, and off the kitchen a screened porch with comfortable furniture overlooks the yard. Guest suites have traditional furnishings such as new four-poster beds and rocking chairs.

The innkeepers, Chip and Penny Kessler, provide helpful notes on local points of interest and restaurants, and the phone booth is well stocked with maps. Breakfast is set out in the dining room where guests help themselves. The Tryon area is famed for the natural beauty of the Blue Ridge Mountains, where a "thermal belt" results in surprisingly warm temperatures and unusually fine crops of apples, grapes, and peaches.

Accommodations: 8 rooms with private bath. *Pets:* Not permitted. *Driving Instructions:* The inn is on Route 108 between Tryon and Exit 36 from I-26.

PINE CREST INN

200 Pine Crest Lane, Tryon, North Carolina. Mailing address: P.O. Box 1030, Tryon, NC 28782. 704-859-9135. *Innkeepers:* Bob and Helene Johnson. Open all year.

Pine Crest Inn is a group of rustic cottages and a lodge in a landscaped setting overlooking Tryon from a secluded hillside at the end of a cul-de-sac surrounded by tall pines, well-manicured grounds, and little walkways leading to the various lodgings. The original buildings date back to 1906, with cottages from the 1920s, 30s, and 40s and a modern house built in 1960. Three of the guest rooms are in a pine-paneled lodge, and all rooms and suites have either a sitting room, fireplace, or both. All are spacious, with pine paneling in most and comfortable rustic furnishings combined with such amenities as air-conditioning and modern baths. The lodge houses a sitting room with couches grouped around the stone fireplace and decorative touches such as antique trunks and hunting prints. A large stone veranda is off this room, as is the dining room, which serves three meals daily to both overnight guests and the public. This paneled room is softly lit by an iron chandelier, candles set on handmade pine trestle tables, and the glow from the wood fire in the large stone fireplace. A chalkboard proclaims the day's menu, the specialties being roasts of beef, pork, and lamb, along with grilled boneless baby salmon.

Accommodations: 31 rooms with private bath. *Pets:* Not permitted. *Driving Instructions:* In Tryon, follow the sign at the railroad crossing on Route 176.

Waynesville, North Carolina

HALLCREST INN

299 Halltop Road, Waynesville, NC 28786. 704-456-6457. *Innkeepers:* Russell and Margaret Burson. Open mid-May through October.

Hallcrest Inn is an 1880s farmhouse near the Balsam Mountain Range in western North Carolina. At an altitude of 3,200 feet on Hall Mountain, it offers sweeping views of valleys and surrounding mountains. The front porch, with its silvery tin roof and tidy row of old granny rockers, is probably the most popular spot for sitting and enjoying the scenery. The farmhouse is set amid tall oaks, lilacs, apple trees, and dogwoods. Guests are welcome to pick raspberries, blackberries, and apples in season.

This is a very casual and informal inn. The guest rooms are simply furnished with family antiques and even come equipped with traditional creaky floors. Two rooms have fireplaces. A motel-type building in the rear houses four additional guest rooms, although we feel our readers will prefer the main house. Meals are served family-style in the dining room, which also has a fireplace. The Bursons make everything fresh right here — even the ice cream, a summer specialty on Saturday nights. The ancient farm bell is rung to announce mealtimes and to bid departing guests "farewell and safe journey."

Accommodations: 12 rooms with private bath. *Pets:* Not permitted. *Driving Instructions:* Take U.S. 276 north from Waynesville, turn left on Mauney Cove Road; then follow signs to the inn, which is south of Route 40.

THE PIEDMONT INN AND MOTOR LODGE

630 Eagles Nest Road, Waynesville, North Carolina. Mailing address: P.O. Box 419, Waynesville, N.C. 28786. 704-456-8636. *Innkeeper:* Jane McKay. Inn open May through October; motor lodge and cottages open all year.

The Piedmont Inn is a small, friendly country resort in the scenic, mountainous "Land of the Sky" region, only a few miles from the Great Smoky Mountains National Park. It sits at an altitude of some 3,000 feet on the 5,000-foot Eagles Nest Mountain. The Piedmont was once the stopping-off place for tourists en route to the famous Eagles Nest Hotel, atop the mountain, which burned in 1916. The inn's property includes about 250 acres just minutes from Waynesville. The grounds offer numerous traditional summer-resort facilities such as a swimming pool, a tennis court, and hiking trails. The inn, a sprawling white building with a long veranda stretching its length, is surrounded by broad lawns shaded by oaks and maples. Several new cottages and a motor lodge are on the property, but the inn proper was built in 1880 with two additions before the turn of the century.

Guest rooms in the inn are simply furnished with country pieces. Three are suitable for the handicapped. The lobby and dining room are casual and warmed by fires in wood-burning stoves on cool evenings and rainy days. A Continental breakfast, the only meal served, is available. Guests wishing rooms in the inn itself must be sure to specify this when making reservations.

Accommodations: 15 rooms in the inn with private bath; 25 in the motor lodge, duplexes, and cottages. *Pets:* Permitted in the motel and cottages but not in the inn. *Driving Instructions:* From Waynesville take Route 19A–U.S. 23 south to the Hazelwood exit (Eagles Nest Road). Turn right and go 1¼ miles to the Piedmont (a sign is on the right).

THE SWAG

Hemphill Road, Waynesville, North Carolina. Mailing address: Route 2, Box 280-A, Waynesville, NC 28786. 704-926-3119; off season: 404-875-1632. *Innkeepers:* Dan and Deener Matthews. Open Memorial Day to late October.

Almost a mile high in the Smoky Mountains, surrounded by acres of mountain meadows and woodlands, stands a mountain inn built of century-old hand-hewn logs and local mountain stone. When Dan and Deener Matthews decided to build their mountain retreat, they first had to construct a gravel road 2.5 miles long to the mountaintop. They dismantled five abandoned antique log buildings and used the salvaged materials to create an inn with nine guest rooms. Another building, Chestnut Lodge, houses a racquetball court, a sauna, a library, three guest rooms, and a living room with a stone fireplace.

The Matthewses have furnished The Swag with arts and crafts of Tennessee and North Carolina as well as with their family antiques. The living room has a cathedral ceiling, exposed-log walls, and a loft with colorful quilts draped over the railings. A player piano with several hundred rolls gets attention during the evening sing-alongs.

Three guest rooms are paneled in old chestnut. Six have fireplaces, and all are provided with patchwork quilts. Fresh fruit, flowers, and terrycloth robes are thoughtfully set out.

Meals at The Swag are served family style on two large tavern tables set with pewter. The entrées are accompanied by fresh vegetables, salads, and home-baked breads and desserts. The inn is in a dry county, but guests may bring their own spirits. Afterward the front porch and an old rocker await, offering the stillness of the mountains under a canopy of stars.

Accommodations: 12 rooms, 11 with private bath and 3 with steam showers. *Pets:* Not permitted. *Driving Instructions:* Take Route 276 north of Waynesville to Hemphill Road. Turn west at the inn's sign and drive to The Swag. This drive is not for the faint of heart. The road has hairpin turns and climbs nearly straight up a very steep mountain.

Wilmington, North Carolina

GRAYSTONE GUEST HOUSE

100 South Third Street, Wilmington, NC 28401. 919-762-0358.
Innkeepers: Rodney G. Perry and D. Gordon Plummer. Open all
year.

This lavish, four-story, 14,000 square foot stone mansion was the talk
of Wilmington back in 1906, when Mrs. Elizabeth Haywood Bridgers
commissioned architect Charles McMillan to design an Italian Renaissance Revival displaying opulent detailing inside and out. The mansion has been completely restored and decorated by two Raleigh interior designers, Rodney G. Perry and D. Gordon Plummer, who purchased the grand structure and transformed it into elegant guest
accommodations. The six guest rooms on the second floor are decorated with formal antiques, plush carpeting, and original artwork.
Several rooms have non-working fireplaces; one room has a canopied
bed, while another features a sleigh bed and early mahogany pieces.

Continental breakfasts are served on fine china and silver in the guests' rooms. The first floor has a sitting room, a library, a music room, and a vast drawing room, all displaying fine antiques and objets d'art.

Graystone Guest House is in the heart of Wilmington's historic district, near boutiques and restaurants. The Cape Fear River is three blocks away, and a park, restored wharf areas, and Cotton Exchange also feature shops, restaurants, and a museum.

Accommodations: 6 rooms, 4 with private bath. *Pets and children:* Not permitted. *Driving Instructions:* The inn is in the historic district of Wilmington just east of the Cape Fear River.

Winston-Salem, North Carolina

COLONEL LUDLOW HOUSE

Summit & West 5th, Winston-Salem, NC 27101. 919-777-1887. *Innkeepers:* H. Kenneth Land. Open all year.

Colonel Ludlow House provides the best of two worlds, a restored Victorian home furnished with period antiques skillfully combined with modern luxuries, such as whirlpool baths for two, stereo systems complete with tape collections, telephones, wet bars, and lots of fresh flowers and greenery. The twentieth-century amenities are tucked into Victorian rooms that include half tester, brass, and carved hardwood bedsteads, Oriental rugs, and period decor. The formal parlor, dining room, and grounds landscaped with pre-1900s plantings make this bed-and-breakfast a popular spot for wedding, anniversary, and birthday celebrations. Colonel Ludlow House, listed in the National Register of Historic Places, is part of the historic West End community of Winston-Salem, within easy walking distance of restaurants, shops, and parks. The restored 1700s Moravian village, Old Salem, is just a mile away. Breakfast is the only meal served.

Accommodations: 9 rooms with private bath. *Pets:* Not permitted. *Driving Instructions:* Take I-40 into Winston-Salem and take the Broad Street-Downtown exit. At the end of the exit ramp, turn right onto Broad Street. At the fourth traffic light, turn left onto West 5th. The inn is at the next traffic light.

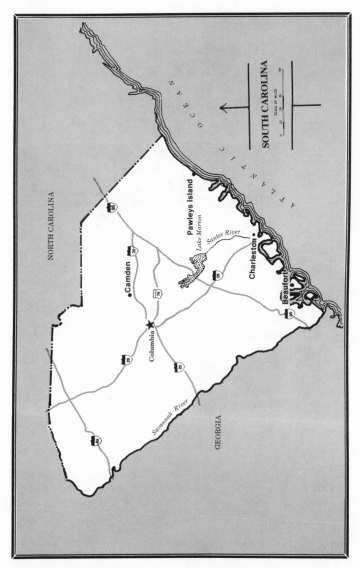

SOUTH CAROLINA

SCALE OF MILES

NORTH CAROLINA

ATLANTIC OCEAN

Pawleys Island

Lake Marion

Santee River

Camden

Charleston

Columbia

Beaufort

Savannah River

GEORGIA

South Carolina

BAY STREET INN

   601 Bay Street, Beaufort, SC 29902. 803-524-7720. *Innkeepers:* Gene and Kathleen Roe. Open all year except August.

The Bay Street Inn is a historic beauty. The antebellum mansion, built in 1852 in the heyday of cotton wealth by a rich plantation owner, Lewis Reave Sams, has been restored and is listed in the National Register of Historic Places. With its large white columns, high ceilings, elaborate woodwork, and fine plasterwork, the house is the epitome of the elegant Beaufort style.

   The inn is at the edge of Beaufort's historic district, "Old Point," and faces the Intracoastal Waterway and the Beaufort River. Almost every window offers a view of the water. Often one can catch glimpses of porpoises frolicking below. In the distance, one can see the bridge connecting the city to the Sea Islands.

   The restoration preserves the original use of each room. Hence, the Library is just that, and the parlors remain parlors complete with their black marble fireplaces. All the rooms are furnished with a variety of antiques from many periods but in keeping with the atmosphere of the inn. French, English, and American antiques are found in the guest rooms, with beds ranging from an elaborate French import to a Carolina rice bed. Each guest room has a fireplace, bath, and sitting area. Fresh seasonal flowers placed in the rooms are replaced in the off season by silk ones.

Breakfasts are served on silver, crystal, and fine china in any spot that catches a guest's fancy, be it porch, library, or garden. For beach excursions or a jaunt to the old church ruins or nearby bird sanctuary, the Roes can arrange for a picnic basket and a private tour with a knowledgeable guide. Bicycles are available for leisurely tours of this interesting Southern port. On your way in and out of the inn, take note of the cracks in the inn's marble steps. The building was occupied during the Civil War, first as an officer's club and later as a Union hospital. It is said that the cracks resulted when the ladies of the house threw trunks off the upper balcony after being warned that union troops were advancing on the city.

Accommodations: 5 rooms with private bath. *Pets and preschool children:* Not permitted. *Driving Instructions:* From Charleston, take Route 17 south to Garden Corners, then Route 21 to Beaufort.

Camden, South Carolina

THE INN

1308 Broad Street, Camden, SC 29020. 803-425-1806. *Innkeeper:* C.E.S. deLoach. Open all year.

Camden, established in 1733, is South Carolina's oldest inland town and the scene of several skirmishes and battles during the Revolutionary War. In addition to historic sites, the area attracts horse lovers, who come to enjoy polo, horse shows, riding trails, and the Carolina Cup and Colonial Cup steeplechase races. The Inn is a complex of historic buildings with twelve guest rooms, each with a color-coordinated private bath. The inn's restaurant, The Veranda, is located in one house and offers a five-entrée menu, with specials such as fresh salmon with tarragon sauce and rib eye au poivre. A Continental breakfast is served to overnight guests only.

Joshua Reynolds House, built in the early nineteenth century, was at one time the office of Abraham Lincoln's brother-in-law, Dr. Todd. Next door is the turn-of-the-century McLean House, which has a staircase with its original brass "dust guards" still in place. The guest rooms and parlors of both houses are decorated with a combination of antiques, period reproductions, and traditional upholstered pieces. There are several with fireplaces, and fresh flowers are the rule.

Accommodations: 12 rooms with private bath. *Pets:* Not permitted. *Driving Instructions:* The inn is just off I-20 in Camden.

along South Battery   Jessie Gerard '86

Charleston, South Carolina

BATTERY CARRIAGE HOUSE

20 South Battery, Charleston, SC 29401. 803-723-9881; toll free: 800-845-7638 (out of state); 800-922-7638 (in South Carolina only). *Innkeepers:* Becky and Frank G. Gay, Jr. Open all year.

Charleston is one of the best-preserved and loveliest cities in America. Its cobblestone streets, fresh sea air, moss-draped oaks, and refined beauty of the homes, gardens, and parks overwhelm even the most jaded of all travelers. In the midst of all this is the Battery Carriage House, an ideal hideaway for visitors wishing to surround themselves with the city's gracious atmosphere. It is tucked behind a mansion built in 1845 in the heart of the historic Battery (pronounced *bah-try*, if you wish to blend in). The mansion is owned and lived in by Frank Gay and his wife, Becky, who have impeccably restored and refurbished the ground floor and Carriage House (formerly the servants' quarters) to house ten guest rooms off the wisteria-covered brick courtyard behind wrought-iron gates. The Gays' mansion looks regally out over the Battery and harbor, and its luxurious guest quarters combine the ambience of the Old South with today's modern conveniences. Out of sight behind discreetly shuttered doors are such amenities as color television, stereo radio, a fully equipped kitchenette, and a bar thoughtfully stocked with chilled soft drinks and a complimentary bottle of wine that is replenished daily. The rooms are decorated with wallpapers and fabrics of historic Charleston. There are Oriental carpets, canopied beds, and eighteenth-century–style furnishings, reproductions of the antiques that graced the many mansions and townhouses of the Old City.

A Continental breakfast of hot coffee, juice, and Benedict cheesecake (a treasured recipe of Becky's family) is served either in the guest rooms or in the walled garden shaded by wisteria vines, with potted flowers adding splashes of color from their brick-wall niches. Guests may have the use of touring bikes for exploring the city. There is also a small, heated swimming pool in the atrium. The Gays will gladly steer guests to favorite restaurants featuring Charleston's unique cuisine. They will also point out the best bike routes, museums, historic sites, and shopping areas. If guests choose to relax and stay close to the Carriage House, there is a service called Moveable Feast that delivers smoked hens, crusty French breads, fruits, cheeses, and other good things to eat. The picnic comes in a split-oak picnic basket and is delivered right to your door.

Accommodations: 10 rooms with private bath. *Driving Instructions:* Take Route 26 to the Meeting Street exit and continue on Meeting Street until you reach the waterfront. The inn is on the right.

ELLIOTT HOUSE INN

78 Queen Street, Charleston, SC 29401. 803-723-1855; toll free: 800-845-7638 (out of state); 800-922-7638 (in South Carolina only). *Innkeeper:* Ann Berdet. Open all year.

The original section of Elliott House goes back almost to the beginnings of Charleston. The first buildings on the property, known in 1800 as Schenkingh's Square, were erected by William Mills, father of

Robert Mills, the architect of the Washington Monument. Elliott House today has been enlarged with the addition of an eighteenth-century-style carriage house encircling an open-air courtyard. Here, period guest rooms open onto individual balconies overlooking a wisteria arbor and the Jacuzzi pool. Many guests enjoy taking their Continental breakfast out on the little tables in the courtyard by the fountain, while others luxuriate with breakfast in bed, which arrives on a silver tray with fresh pastries, chilled orange juice, and a pot of steaming coffee or tea. Afternoon tea is served in the garden.

Each room is decorated, in keeping with the inn's atmosphere, with canopied beds and handsome armoires. The latter not only hold one's belongings during a stay at Elliott House but also conceal the room's color-television set. The inn's furnishings, styled in the manner of the eighteenth century, are beautifully set off by the coordinated wall coverings and fabrics typical of historic Charleston. All rooms have telephones and daily complimentary bottles of wine.

Elliott House has bicycles for guests' use. For those who enjoy it, cycling is one of the best ways to see the many historic and picturesque sights of this lovely old city. A block to the west of the inn is King Street, the antiquing district. Going a block in the opposite direction brings one to the cobblestones and gaslights of Chalmers Street.

Accommodations: 26 rooms with private bath. *Driving Instructions:* Exit off I-26 at Meeting Street, continue south to Queen Street, turn right on Queen Street, and go half a block to the inn.

INDIGO INN

1 Maiden Lane, Charleston, SC 29401. 803-577-5900. *Innkeeper:* Faye Neal. Open all year.

In the eighteenth century, indigo was the king of the crops, its deep elegant blue desired the world over. "Carolina Blue" was much sought after, being the finest of the Lowcountry dyes. The splendor of the era of indigo harvests has been recaptured at the Indigo Inn, a re-creation (1979) of an eighteenth-century building where lush, greenery-bedecked balconies open onto a peaceful courtyard. The emphasis of the decor is on the intensely colorful fabrics inspired by indigo dyes.

The inn's rooms feature many graceful pieces of mahogany furniture, period antiques, and reproductions. The lobby displays Oriental rugs and eighteenth-century pieces and has softly lit paneled walls. The inn's popular "Hunt" breakfast is served here buffet style on the antique sideboard. Ham biscuits are among the favorite offerings, along with three kinds of homemade breads and compotes of fresh fruit in season. The guest rooms are built around the inn's courtyard and almost all have queen-size beds. Cannonball beds and the famous Charleston rice beds are in many of the rooms.

The Indigo Inn is in the very heart of Charleston's historic district; from the inn's cobblestone entranceway, guests are but a short distance from the Market area, with its little shops, eateries, and open-air markets. The inn recently expanded its facilities to include Jasmine House, an 1840 building across the street, which has six suites for bed and breakfast.

Accommodations: 46 rooms with private bath. *Driving Instructions:* The inn is near the corner of Meeting and Pinckney streets.

PLANTERS INN

Market at Meeting Street, Charleston, SC 29401. 803-722-2345.
Innkeeper: Robert D. Albert. Open all year.
Overlooking historic Charleston's eighteenth-century marketplace is the Planters Inn, housed in a meticulously renovated 1840 commercial structure, restored under guidelines set by the U.S. Department of Interior. The original facade, masonry, and other significant arcitectural details were carefully preserved, along with the columns and cornices, which were reconstructed or refurbished as needed. Within these historic walls is an elegant urban inn with the look and feel of

one of Charleston's fine antebellum estates. The lobby is furnished with eighteenth-century antiques and reproductions modeled after historic Charleston pieces. The guest rooms and suites have pieces from the same period, including mahogany four-poster beds, chaise longues, and high windows draped in swags. Behind the historic exterior is a full-service hotel, with special French milled soaps, plush pillows, and nightly turn-down service that includes extra pillows and Italian chocolates left at the bedside.

The inn's restaurant, Silks, was named for the inn's collection of racing silks and equestrian artwork. Highlights of the menu include game, such as venison, quail, and duck, as well as beef and seafood dishes, along with an extensive list of American and imported wines.

Accommodations: 43 rooms with private bath. *Pets:* Not permitted. *Driving Instructions:* Exit off I-26 onto Meeting Street to downtown and take Market Street. The inn is on the corner of Meeting and Market streets.

SWEET GRASS INN

23 Vendue Range, Charleston, SC 29401. 803-577-7970; toll free: 800-845-7900 (out of state). *Innkeepers:* Evelyn and Morton Needle; managed by the Vendue Inn. Open all year.

The Sweet Grass Inn is in the French Quarter of Charleston. It sits halfway between the Battery and the Market in the historic waterfront district once lined with warehouses. The inn was named for the low-country grasses used by the "little basket ladies" of South Carolina in weaving their baskets.

Built around 1800, the Sweet Grass Inn has been restored and decorated by the Needles family. The old woodwork, pegged beams, and wide-board pine flooring are set off by bright white walls. The inn is furnished with antiques and family treasures, and the living-room fireplace has a mantel of deep-swamp cypress. Guests at the Sweet Grass Inn are treated to thoughtful little personal touches such as fresh flowers and small baskets of fruit. On sunny days breakfast is served on a roof terrace that overlooks Charleston harbor.

Accommodations: 8 rooms with private bath. *Pets:* Not permitted. *Driving Instructions:* From Savannah, Georgia, take I-95 and then Route 61 to Lockwood Boulevard in Charleston. Turn left on Calhoun, and then turn right on East Bay Street and drive to Vendue Range.

SWORD GATE INN

111 Tradd Street, Charleston, SC 29401. 803-723-8518. *Innkeeper:* Walter Benton. Open all year.

The Sword Gate Inn is in one wing of Sword Gate House in the heart of Charleston's large historic district. The main house was built in the mid-eighteenth century. In the 1820s it was used as a French boarding school for girls; and in the 1850s, as a British consulate.

The rooms, formerly the servants' quarters, are furnished simply with comfortable beds and antiques scattered here and there. Three rooms have high four-poster beds, and the four contains a fabric-covered bedstead. Coverlets and sheets reflect the changing seasons; in spring there are bright floral prints on white backgrounds, and in fall the colors are warm oranges and golds. Comforters lie across the beds.

Charleston breakfasts are offered in the courtyard or the formal dining room. Guests help themselves to coffee, juice, fruits, and coddled eggs. Every day there are lots of sweet rolls and grits. Wine and cheese are served in the evenings.

Guests are given a tour of the ballroom, a fine example of gracious Charleston architecture. Elaborate moldings and the fireplace's carved mantels are enhanced by the ornate crystal-and-frosted-glass chandelier that hangs from the center-ceiling medallion with its gilded oak-cluster design. At the top of the house is a spacious, antique-filled bedroom with a canopied bed, its delicately crocheted top of tobacco twine. It is the special honeymoon suite. Bicycles are available.

Accommodations: 6 rooms with private bath. *Pets:* Not permitted. *Children:* Under six not permitted. *Driving Instructions:* Too complicated to describe here. Get directions from the innkeeper.

TWO MEETING STREET INN

2 Meeting Street, Charleston, SC 29401. 803-723-7322. *Innkeeper:* David S. Spell. Open all year.

When Martha Williams became the bride of Waring P. Carrington in 1890, her wealthy father gave her a check for $75,000 set on a rose-colored cushion. It was to build the newlyweds a Queen Anne Victorian home. During the two years it took to build the house, known today as the Two Meeting Street Inn, the couple traveled extensively in Europe. The Carringtons donated the columned bandstand in the park across the street from the inn so that they could enjoy concerts without leaving the comfort of their piazza. They lived here for more than half a century and entertained distinguished guests from all over the world, including Princess Anastasia of Russia and Warren G. Harding before his presidency. In 1946, the inn was purchased by the Carr family and was run for many years as a guest house by Mrs. Carr, aunt of the present owner.

The inn is surrounded on two sides by arched piazzas facing Battery Park to capture the southern breezes. Standing in the large entrance foyer, one can see magnificent Tiffany stained-glass windows in the living room, dining room, foyer, and on the stair landing. A built-in china cabinet containing some of the innkeeper's collection of blue and white Canton china graces one wall in the oval dining room. Over the cabinet is a sunburst stained-glass window measuring some 6 feet across.

The inn is furnished with family antiques, silver, crystal, Oriental rugs, and period pieces. Five bedrooms branch off the upstairs foyer, and two smaller bedrooms sharing two baths are on the third floor. Three bedrooms open onto an upstairs piazza, and one of the two Honeymoon Suites has its own balcony.

The inn's corner lot has several live oak trees more than a hundred

years old. A Continental breakfast is served in the dining room, on the piazza, or out in the gardens.

Accommodations: 7 rooms, 5 with private bath; including 2 suites. *Pets:* Not permitted. *Children:* Only well-behaved teenagers permitted. *Driving Instructions:* From I-26 or U.S. 17 exit onto Meeting Street and drive to the end of the street. The inn is at the corner of South Battery Street.

VENDUE INN

19 Vendue Range, Charleston, SC 29401. 803-577-7970; toll-free: 800-845-7900 (out of state), 800-922-7900 (in South Carolina).

Innkeepers: Evelyn and Morton Needle. Open all year.

The Vendue Inn is a fine example of urban restoration. Evelyn and Morton Needle, with years of experience in the construction business, located a structurally sound, handsome warehouse near Cooper River. Recognizing the beauty of the old pine floors and arched windows, they set out to create an intimate inn in the tradition of Southern hospitality. The guest rooms that emerged are each differently decorated with reproductions of period furniture. There are four-postered canopy beds, brass beds, reproduction lighting, Oriental rugs, pine chests, and comfortable stuffed chairs. Each room is named after a noteworthy South Carolinian, with a biographical sketch providing a miniature history lesson as a bonus.

The inn uses attractive linen throughout, and all the rooms have coordinated drapes and bedspreads. The wallpapers in the guest rooms are reproduction striped-floral early prints, with gay floral patterns in the bathrooms. Each room has a complete modern bathroom, color television, and central air conditioning. Beds are turned down nightly and foil-wrapped mints placed on the pillows, and in the morning a butler brings a Continental breakfast. The Needles provide guests with bicycles for sightseeing excursions. In the afternoon, wine and cheese is served in the indoor courtyard, which is festooned with hanging and potted plants. Often visiting chamber artists or members of the Charleston Symphony Orchestra play music for guests. A restaurant featuring low-country fare is planned for mid-1985.

Accommodations: 18 rooms with private bath. *Pets:* Not permitted. *Driving Instructions:* Take I-26 or Route 701-17 to the center of Charleston, exiting at Meeting Street. Drive south on Meeting Street to Cumberland, turn left (east) on Cumberland to East Bay Street. Turn right and drive one long block to Vendue Range, the extension of Queen Street, which runs one way to the west.

Pawleys Island, South Carolina

SEA VIEW INN

Pawleys Island, SC 29585. 803-237-4253. *Innkeeper:* Page Oberlin. Open May through October.

Pawleys Island, off the coast of South Carolina's plantation low country, is simple, unspoiled, and uncrowded. In the late eighteenth century wealthy plantation families would come here in the summer months to escape the heat. Their summer plantations, surrounded by moss-covered oaks and lovely gardens, are still here. And so are the unchanged salt marshes, high dunes, and waving beach grasses.

Sea View Inn is as unspoiled as her island. It's a low-keyed family inn, a haven of uncomplicated pleasures, overlooking the salt marshes and sea. Its central courtyard takes full advantage of the ocean breezes, and the large, airy guest rooms all look out to sea. Here white curtains flutter and the salt-bleached unfinished floors are smooth to bare feet. The living room is big and sunny, with bright chintz slipcovers on soft overstuffed furniture. Vases of fresh flowers share space with collections of shells on coffee tables and the fireplace mantel. A well-stocked library lines one wall.

Sea View Inn specializes in seafood and low-country food. An evening meal might include among its many offerings a deviled-crab gumbo, black-eyed peas, and spoonbread, or scalloped oysters, corn casserole, and peach cobbler with hard sauce.

After a day of clamming, crabbing, swimming, or bird watching combined with one of Sea View's meals, what could be better than settling into one of the old rocking chairs on the veranda or strolling the quiet beach.

Accommodations: 18 rooms with half bath and shared showers. *Pets:* Not permitted. *Children:* Under three not permitted. *Driving Instructions:* Take Route 17 south of Myrtle Beach for 30 miles.

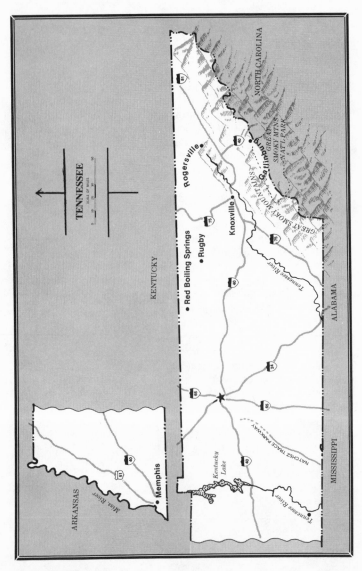

Tennessee

Gatlinburg, Tennessee

BUCKHORN INN

Tudor Mountain Road, Gatlinburg, TN 37738. 615-436-4668. *Innkeeper:* Kathy Welch. Open all year except December.

On a peaceful hilltop, less than a mile from the Greenbriar entrance to the Great Smoky Mountains National Park, is the Buckhorn Inn. Secluded by tall pines and shade trees on 30 acres of landscaped lawns and untouched woodlands, the inn has views of the greens and soft purples of the highest peaks of the Smokies (up to 6,500 feet).

Buckhorn Inn was built in 1938 near a spring-fed lake. In the woods around the lake are guest cottages, each with a porch, a stone fireplace in its living room, and a bedroom and bath. At the inn itself, lounge chairs line the colonnaded porch. Guest rooms inside are furnished with antiques, and each has air conditioning and a private bath. The inn's living room is an inviting place, with bookshelves and a stone fireplace. A piano awaits musically inclined guests, and a round coffee table is drawn up to comfortable couches. Large potted plants add touches of greenery from their stands in front of the sunny windows and French doors. The dining room is set with fresh linens and candles for the evening meals, available only to guests at the inn. In winter dinner is served only on weekends.

Accommodations: 7 rooms and 4 cottages with private bath. *Pets and preschool children:* Not permitted. *Driving Instructions:* Take I-441 to Gatlinburg, turn east on U.S. 321, and drive 5 miles to Buckhorn Road. Turn left on Buckhorn, drive ¾ mile to Tudor Mountain Road, and turn right.

WONDERLAND HOTEL

Route 2, Gatlinburg, TN 37738. 615-436-5490. *Innkeeper:* Darrell
Huskey. Open Memorial Day weekend through October.

Within the Great Smoky Mountains National Park is a rustic, wonderful old hotel offering an old-fashioned vacation with little to disturb the quiet but the whispering wind through the trees, the songs of
birds, and the sounds of the river rushing down the Little River Gorge
just 75 yards away. Built in 1912, the hotel has changed very little over
the years. The wide veranda still has its row of rocking chairs where
guests visit and relax, with views of the Smokies. Inside there is a large
sitting area around the fireplace, a game room with Ping-Pong and
card tables, and guest rooms that are simply furnished. The dining
room serves three meals a day to both overnight guests and the public.
Dinnertime favorites include fried chicken and country ham.

For the more energetic, the hotel provides inner tubes for floating
on the river. There is a natural swimming hole nearby, and more than
700 miles of marked trails throughout the park.

Accommodations: 26 rooms, 13 with private bath. *Pets:* Not permitted. *Driving Instructions:* Take Route 441 south. Two miles from
Gatlinburg, take Route 73 west and drive 4¾ miles to a sign giving
directions to the inn.

Knoxville, Tennessee

THREE CHIMNEYS OF KNOXVILLE

1302 White Avenue, Knoxville, TN 37916. 615-521-4970. *Innkeepers:* Alfred and Margo Ackerman. Open all year.

We discovered Three Chimneys just in time for the 1982 World's Fair. This pretty, shingled Queen Anne mansion was built in 1896 in the Knoxville neighborhood of Fort Sanders, where author James Agee once lived. The inn has five large, carpeted guest rooms furnished with Victorian pieces. Two rooms have fireplaces with tiling around them. These fireplaces were built to burn coal, but one has been adapted for wood-burning. Each of the guest rooms is named for a wildflower or other plant of the nearby Great Smoky Mountains region.

Guests at Three Chimneys enjoy a Southern breakfast in the glassed-in porch on the east side of the house. On warm, sunny days they can sit on the roof porch overlooking other homes of the neighborhood, many of which are listed in the National Register of Historic Places. The sloping backyard is bounded by a wall of mountain stone. A lily pond reflects a large white dogwood tree and a Southern magnolia.

Accommodations: 5 rooms, 3 with private bath. *Pets:* Not permitted. *Driving Instructions:* The inn is at Thirteenth Street and White Avenue.

LOWENSTEIN-LONG HOUSE

217 N. Waldran, Memphis, TN 38105. 901-527-7174. *Innkeeper:* Martha Long. Open all year.

This stone mansion was built at the turn of the century by Abraham Lowenstein, founder of the Lowenstein Department Store. The four-story "late Victorian" was a showcase for the very best that money could buy: Stained glass windows, marble-walled baths and kitchen, tooled-leather wall coverings, and the finest wood and plaster crafts-manship. In the 1920s the estate was sold to the Beethoven Music Club, which held recitals in the grand conservatory room, the drawing room, and the music room, all on the first floor. Music lessons were given on the second floor, while the third floor housed practice rooms. It was sold again in the 1940s and, after a series of owners, fell into disrepair.

The Longs rescued the mansion and, after much hard work, opened the Lowenstein-Long House to overnight guests. Now listed in the National Register of Historic Places, it has been nominated for a preservation award by the city of Memphis. The enormous rooms are furnished with a combination of Victorian and comfortable modern pieces. The woodwork and elaborate plaster cornices have been restored, and some of the baths still retain the original marble walls. A Continental breakfast is served in the dining room.

Accommodations: 6 rooms, 5 with private bath. *Pets:* Not permitted. *Driving Instructions:* From I-240, take the Madison, Union, or Front Street exits to Poplar Avenue. The inn is on North Waldran, just north of Poplar Avenue, near downtown Memphis.

Red Boiling Springs, Tennessee

DONOHO HOTEL

East Main Street, Red Boiling Springs, Tennessee. Mailing address: P.O. Box 36, Red Boiling Springs, TN 37150. 615-699-3141. *Innkeepers:* Patrick and Edith Walsh. Open May through September.

Red Boiling Springs had its heyday in the Roaring Twenties when people flocked from all over to partake of the cure-all waters of the springs. At that time there were eight or nine hotels and numerous tourist homes serving the health-seeking tourists. Despite this, many visitors could not be accommodated and had to sleep in their cars. Several of these hotels burned over the years, including one with the rather cheerless name of Deadman Hotel.

Unlike its peers, the Donoho Hotel is still going strong today, in spite of a definite decline in the tourist trade about town. Built in 1914, it is a traditional old-fashioned summer resort hotel with a long, colonnaded two-story porch, complete with comfortable rocking chairs. Tall shade trees grace the lawn where wooden lawn chairs are arranged. Many of the area's attractions remain, including its lovely lakes, a golf course, a swimming pool, and tennis courts in the village.

Innkeeper Edith Walsh confides, however, that the main attraction at the Donoho is its big front-porch rockers where, after a good meal in the hotel dining room, folks simply like to sit, talk, and rock while waiting for the next mealtime to roll around.

There is every reason for anticipation concerning meals. The Donoho is famous for its no-menu, family-style, all-you-can-eat dining. The big dinner bell rings three times daily, at 8 A.M., noon, and 5 P.M. At lunch and dinner each table in the old-fashioned dining room is filled with large bowls of a variety of vegetables and large plates of country ham, fried chicken, or roast beef. Heaps of hot homemade biscuits accompany the meal, and pots of honey and preserves are always on hand. The bowls and platters are refilled as needed until the meal is over. The dining room is open to the public, but reservations are advised. For houseguests, two or three meals daily are included in the room rate.

Inside the hotel, one is transported back in time to a gentler era when the pace was slower. Ceiling paddle-fans still lazily push the air about, and hand-painted shades adorn the hanging lamps in the public rooms. Downstairs are a gift shop, a lobby, and a music room containing the hotel's television and piano. Guest rooms here are simply yet comfortably furnished with antique pieces as well as traditional summer hotel furniture.

Guests who wish to sample one of the three kinds of mineral waters at Red Boiling Springs (there used to be five) need only stroll across the wooden footbridge spanning Salt Lick Creek.

Accommodations: 44 rooms, 36 with private bath. *Driving Instructions:* From Lafayette, take Route 52 to Red Boiling Springs.

Rogersville, Tennessee

HALE SPRINGS INN

Town Square, Rogersville, TN 37857. 615-272-5171. *Innkeepers:* Sheldon and Marlina Livesay. Open all year.

The historic little town of Rogersville in the hills of eastern Tennessee was founded in 1786 on land that was a wedding gift to Joseph Rogers and his bride. Davy Crockett's grandparents had a cabin on Crockett Creek, which runs through town, and the Crocketts and the Rogerses are all buried in the old town cemetery. In 1824, Hale Springs Inn was built on Main Street and has been in business ever since, making it the oldest inn in continuous operation in Tennessee. In the Civil War it served as the Union headquarters. Andrew Jackson lived in the hotel for a spell, and over the years it was visited by two more presidents.

It was only natural someone would come along and tackle the renovation of this historic inn. That someone was the former innkeeper, Carl Netherland-Brown, previously a captain of the liner SS Bahama Star, who purchased the inn and undertook its restoration. The oldest section was furnished with antiques and rugs of the early nineteenth century, and wallpapers were found that closely approximate those of the period. Several guest rooms have fireplaces, and some, four-poster beds.

The dining room is decorated with Colonial furnishings and has two working fireplaces. Candlelight meals are served to the public, with roast beef the house specialty. Hawkins County is dry, so guests should bring their own spirits.

Accommodations: 10 rooms with private bath. *Pets:* Not permitted, but a kennel is nearby. *Driving Instructions:* Rogersville is halfway between Knoxville and Bristol on Route 11.

HISTORIC RUGBY, INC.

Central Avenue, Rugby, Tennessee. Mailing address: P.O. Box 8, Rugby, TN 37733. 615-628-2441. Open all year except 2 weeks at Christmas.

Rugby, a tiny English-style hamlet, is in the heart of Tennessee's Cumberland Mountains. In 1966 area residents banded together to restore and preserve this historic town, which was founded in 1880 by English author and social reformer Thomas Hughes. He designed and built this community as a cultural cooperative where he felt that young Englishmen in America could channel their energies into agricultural and manual trades. The community was carefully planned with parks, lawn tennis, and about seventy Victorian buildings. Rugby prospered for a few short years; but severe winters, a typhoid epidemic in 1881, and the tendency of the young men to prefer cultural events and high tea to work all contributed to the demise of Hughes's dream.

Although many of the original buildings burned in the last century, today the townspeople are dedicated to the restoration of the remaining buildings and the reconstruction of others. Guides to Historic Rugby list the restored buildings open to the public and include maps of trails throughout the surrounding park. Pioneer Cottage, built in 1880 as the first frame house in Rugby, has been restored and is now available to overnight guests. Originally it was called the "Asylum," for it provided temporary shelter for many early settlers, including Thomas Hughes himself. Newbury House Inn, a recent restoration, is Rugby's first "public house." A nice counterpoint to the more rustic Pioneer Cottage, it has been restored and furnished with more formal Victorian pieces. Guests are served morning and evening tea in the 1880 parlor with its ceiling fans, fireplaces, and Victorian library.

Accommodations: 8 rooms, 3 with private bath. *Pets:* Not permitted. *Driving Instructions:* Historic Rugby is on Route 52, about 60 miles northwest of Knoxville.

Texas

DRISKILL HOTEL

117 East Seventh Street, Austin, TX 78701. 512-474-5911. Open all year.

The Driskill first opened its doors in the 1890s as one of the finest hotels in the Southwest. Rooms, at $2.50 to $5.00 a day, were said to be "First Class in all Appointments!" Today the prices have crept up a bit, but the hotel is still "First Class." It was built by a Texas cattle baron, Colonel J. L. Driskill, at a time when his cattle outnumbered the people of Austin. No expense has been spared in keeping up the atmosphere and trappings of this lavish Romanesque Texas-style hotel. Victorian sofas, chairs, and side tables are set on large expanses of red carpeting in the public rooms, where dark-polished paneled ceilings and woodwork highlight the tapestry wall coverings and antique oil paintings. One of the dining rooms, the Maximilian Room, was designed to display the hotel's unique collection of gold-leaf mirrors that were a wedding gift from Mexico's Emperor

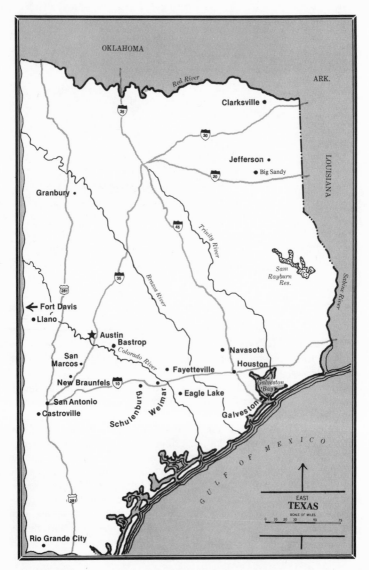

EAST
TEXAS
SCALE OF MILES
0   10   20   30   50   75

Maximilian to his bride, Carlotta. Many of the rooms and suites have been completely restored to Victorian elegance, with marble-topped bureaus, heavy carved period bedsteads and armoires, and brass paddle fans. The most impressive is the L.B.J. Suite, dedicated by Lady Bird Johnson a few years ago. The hotel management is in the process of converting more of the traditional rooms to their antique versions, although the traditional rooms are also quite appealing, and many offer fine views of the city. All meals are served to guests and the public.

Accommodations: 185 rooms with private bath. *Driving Instructions:* Take I-35 to the First–Fifth Street exit. Turn left on Sixth Street and then right on Congress, which leads to Seventh Street.

THE PFEIFFER HOUSE

1802 Main Street, Bastrop, TX 78602. 512-321-2100. *Innkeepers:* Charles and Marilyn Whites. Open all year.

The town of Bastrop recently celebrated its 150th birthday, making it one of the oldest villages in Texas. It is a small, sleepy place, with many fine old houses set along shady streets, an old-fashioned drug store complete with soda fountain, and a vintage 5¢ & 10¢ store. Just down Main Street, on a large corner lot flanked by several big shade trees, is the Pfeiffer House, a gingerbread Victorian "Carpenter Gothic" built in 1901, now listed in the National Register of Historic Places. The Whites are proud of their home and have opened its antique-filled rooms to overnight guests. Bedrooms include handmade quilts, fruit baskets, homemade cookies set out on a tray, and bouquets of fresh flowers. One room has a half-tester bed and a sitting area. Charles and Marilyn make guests feel right at home, inviting them to use the inn's several public rooms, which are filled with books, bric-a-brac, and more family antiques. A full breakfast is served in the dining room. Out in the yard, the clucking sounds of chickens and the buzz of hummingbirds belie the inn's town location.

Accommodations: 3 rooms with shared baths. *Pets and children under 10:* Not permitted. *Driving Instructions:* From Austin, take Route 71 east. Take Business Loop 150 directly to Main Street. The Pfeiffer House is seven blocks north.

Big Sandy, Texas

ANNIE'S BED AND BREAKFAST

Highway 155 North, Big Sandy, Texas. Mailing address: P.O. Box 928, Big Sandy, TX 75755. 214-636-4355. *Innkeepers:* Chris and Jolinda Klotz. Open all year.

Annie's Bed and Breakfast is part of a Big Sandy empire. Many readers may be familiar with Annie's Attic, a thriving mail-order needlepoint business. In addition, there is Annie's Tea Parlor, a popular restaurant; Annie's Gift Shop, offering turn-of-the-century items; and Annie's Needlepoint Gallery, a showcase of the craft items available from Annie's Attic. The bed-and-breakfast inn is located in the Tohill House, a seven-gabled, Victorian-style building with spindle-and-lattice enclosed, upper-and-lower story porches, deep green lawns, and a profusion of blooms in the gardens bordering the house. One guest room, the Queen Victoria room on the main floor, has a richly hued Oriental rug, antique armoire, brass bed topped with a red satin comforter, and a handsome mantel surrounding the fireplace. Upstairs, the Queene Anne room is an attic suite with its own spiral staircase leading to a loft, red wall-to-wall carpeting, and a quilt over a hand-crocheted bedspread, both from the Annie's Attic. Guests may have all their meals, if they wish, right across the street at Annie's Tea Room, which offers Continental and complete breakfasts, luncheons, and dinners that include prime ribs, roast tenderloin of beef, Alaskan salmon, and chicken Florentine. Desserts are a specialty, especially the white chocolate mousse and the pecan pie.

Accommodations: 13 guest rooms, 8 with private bath. *Pets:* Not permitted. *Driving Instructions:* Take Route 155 north of I-20 to Big Sandy, just off U.S. Route 80.

Castroville, Texas

LANDMARK INN STATE HISTORIC SITE

U.S. 90 and Florence Street, Castroville, Texas. Mailing address: P.O. Box 577, Castroville, TX 78009. 512-538-2133. Open all year; park hours: 8–8.

The Landmark Inn is a venerable Texas inn recently acquired by the Texas Parks and Wildlife Department, which operates it as a functioning inn within the setting of a state park. Erected in three sections from 1848 to 1870, the Landmark Inn reflects the cultural heritage and tradition of its builders, immigrant settlers from Alsace-Lorraine. The buildings resemble European Alsatian farmhouses with uniquely Southwestern architectural variations. All are built of native limestone and have 15- to 18-inch plastered walls. The banister of the stairs leading to the upper balcony is made of one continuous piece of cypress. A detached bathhouse had a lead-lined upper story that was used to provide hot baths for guests in the 1850s. According to tradition, the lead was melted into Confederate bullets during the Civil War. From 1867 to 1870, the large downstairs room with hand-hewn doors of pecan wood was the Castroville post office. Slots for mail may still be seen in the doors. The inn's Room 5 served as the Western Union office when cotton was the area's major crop. Most of the guest rooms are adjacent to the upper gallery of the original hotel and overlook a landscaped courtyard and the old Grist Mill that is part of the historic site. The stone buildings filter out highway sounds and create a tranquil atmosphere. Perhaps this tranquillity attracted Robert E. Lee to the inn as a guest a century ago. In restoring the guest rooms, care was taken to make good use of the inn's collection of Texas antiques. The state bought furnishings that would reflect the various ownerships of the inn through the years.

Park property surrounding the Landmark Inn is open to the public for tours and includes a collection of Alsatian-style buildings that reflect the area's many French-Alsatian settlers. Other Alsatian buildings of interest include the *Lutheran Youth Building*, constructed in 1849 as a store; the *Carle House and store*; the *Nicholas Haby House*; and the *Keifer House* (1870). Many of these pioneer homes are open during the spring in even-numbered years.

Accommodations: 8 rooms, 4 with private bath. *Pets:* Permitted on leash on park grounds but *not* overnight. *Driving Instructions:* Travel west on Route 90, turning left immediately after crossing the Medina River in Castroville.

Clarksville, Texas

PECAN INN

Route 6, Clarksville, Texas. Mailing address: Box 642, Clarksville, TX 75426. 214-427-5507. *Innkeepers:* Lib and Sharon Henderson. Open March through December.

Pecan Inn is a mid-nineteenth century homestead surrounded by seven acres of beautiful old pecan trees and a small lake for fishing. Innkeepers Sharon and Lib Henderson can provide horses for riding, a brisk game of croquet, or a shady porch for visiting with fellow guests. The house is furnished with antiques and family mementoes. Dolls decorate the guest rooms as well as the more formal Victorian parlor and living room. Guest rooms have antique beds with quilts and afghans draped over antique oak stands. Claw-footed tubs and sinks are right in three of the rooms. Lib and Sharon offer lemonade and cheese and crackers to guests in the afternoon and their freshly baked pecan pie later in the evening. A full Southern breakfast is served in the dining room.

Accommodations: 4 rooms, 3 with private bath. *Children under 6:* Not permitted. *Driving Instructions:* From Texarkana, take I-30 to Route 82 west. Drive approximately 40 miles to Clarksville. Take Route 37 north one mile and turn left on Old Albion Road. The inn is the first 2-story house on the right.

Eagle Lake, Texas

THE FARRIS 1912

201 North McCarty Avenue, Eagle Lake, TX 77434. 409-234-2546.
Innkeepers: William and Helyn Farris. Open all year, but no
rooms are available in the main building in July and August.

The year 1912 was part of the golden age of Eagle Lake, a time that
saw the town bustling with travelers who had converged there via
three railways. Today the town is quieter and is known as the "goose-
hunting capital of the world." It was in 1912 that the Farris was built,
and all of its furnishings are from that era or earlier. The lobby and
parlors at the Farris contain a mix of white wicker pieces and more
formal upholstered Victorian chairs and settees. Green plants and
flowers abound, and paddle fans turn gently on warm days. The sixteen guest rooms in the main building have fancy iron beds, high-back
oaken beds, and older Victorian four-posters. The Governor's Suite
has a canopied bed. Most bedrooms have patchwork spreads, lace
curtains, and frilly dust ruffles. For guests who prefer a separate
building with first-floor rooms, there is a detached 1920s guest house
where most furnishings date from the early twentieth century.

During the winter hunting season, the inn serves three meals a day
to guests and the public. Food is available the rest of the year when the
guest load warrants. House specialties include pork chops with cherry
sauce, coq-au-vin, plum bread pudding, and pecan pie. Both Farris
buildings stand behind tall Spanish gates. Within the courtyard is a
large carved stone fountain, near which are outdoor tables and chairs.

Accommodations: 24 rooms, 8 with private bath. *Pets:* Not permitted. *Children:* Under twelve permitted in guest house only.
Driving Instructions: From I-10 take exit 720 at Sealy. Drive south 1
mile to FM 3013, and continue on that road to Eagle Lake.

COUNTRY PLACE HOTEL

"On the Square," Fayetteville, TX 78940. 409-378-2712. *Innkeepers:* Clovis and Maryann Heimsath. Open all year.

Fayetteville (population 400) is in the heart of Texas's "bluebonnet country," where every April millions of wildflowers blanket the ground. Since the turn of the century, the Zapp Building has stood beside the village square here. Clovis and Maryann Heimsath, searching for a country place for their architectural firm, fell in love with the landmark brick building and immediately purchased it. Both Heimsaths are artistic in many areas, and they set about restoring and decorating their find. It was soon evident that the building could easily house more than their firm, and so was born the Country Place Hotel. This was not the first time the Zapp Building had welcomed lodgers. In its long career it had served as a department store, a hospital, and a boardinghouse for drummers. Maryann and Clovis took the best room, the second-floor corner balcony room, and converted it to the hotel's parlor. The feeling was it was far too nice a room not to be shared by all the guests. This room is airy with refreshingly spare furnishings: antique wicker and unadorned arched windows overlooking the square. The hotel has two second-floor verandas, one running across the front and the other overlooking a little garden out back with a fountain. A few village skeptics, informing visitors about the hotel, will thoughtfully warn that the furnishings are "kind of old." The "kind of old" furniture is an eclectic blend of old-fashioned pieces, some Victorian carved walnut beds and bureaus and others painted in keeping with the hotel's age. All the beds are covered with handmade patchwork quilts, and even the "air conditioning" is old-fashioned — big old paddle fans overhead.

On the ground floor are the Heimsaths' offices, the lobby and its antique furnishings, and the hotel's restaurant, Country Place, which is open to the public. Sigrid Liehr, who trained in Europe, serves Continental fare for Saturday dinner and Sunday brunch and serves breakfast on Saturdays and Sundays only. Run by two of the innkeepers' friends, Perry and Carol Thacker, it is open Fridays, Saturdays, and Sundays all year. Each day a special menu is offered. Fridays are Mexican, Saturday nights are entirely devoted to gourmet preparations, and Sundays brunch is served. There are several cafés in town for meals not offered by the hotel. The Country Place Hotel is a re-creation of a bygone institution — the old drummer hotel of the kind once found in many railroad towns across the country.

Accommodations: 8 rooms with 2 hall baths. *Driving Instructions:* The hotel is midway between Austin and Houston, 6 miles north of Route 71.

THE LICKSKILLET INN

Fayette Street, Fayetteville, Texas. Mailing address: P.O. Box 85, Fayetteville, TX 78940. 409-378-2846. *Innkeepers:* Steve and Jeanette Donaldson. Open all year.

The Lickskillet Inn and the tiny Texas town of Fayetteville appear to be unchanged by the years. But the house, built in 1852 at the corner of the town square, has undergone some updating since its early days. For one thing, its old central "dog run" — the equivalent of an Easterner's breezeway — is now enclosed and doubles as a hallway and a display area for the Donaldsons' many antiques. Just off the "run" are the inn's guest rooms. Each is decorated with antiques and has many appealing personal touches such as crocheted doilies, knickknacks, and perhaps an old hand mirror or someone's well-loved doll. The rooms have paddle fans, pot-bellied stoves that the Donaldsons will light on cool evenings, and antique beds covered with quilts and crocheted pillow shams. Guests are told the rules of the house when they arrive: Wet towels in the hamper, no smoking, fragile quilts in the armoire at night, and first one up plugs in the coffeepot. Innkeepers and guests eat together in the dining room, where guests are served homemade breads with jams and local honeys with their meals. Jeanette Donaldson is well versed in local lore and enjoys helping people plan their day's explorations.

Accommodations: 4 rooms with shared bath. *Pets and children:* Not permitted. *Driving Instructions:* Fayetteville is 15 miles east of La Grange on Route 159.

THE VICTORIAN INN

511 Seventeenth Street, Galveston, TX 77550. 409-762-3235. Open all year.

In 1889, Isaac Hefron built one of the most striking homes in Galveston. Its bright white and rust-red exterior has three separate balconies and a curved wraparound porch. The superior craftsmanship Hefron insisted on is well preserved in the interior. Five fireplaces boast carved oak mantels and are inset with Belgian tiles. Stair railings show skillful carving, and much of the inn's original stained glass is still intact.

Spacious guest rooms have been individually decorated with a variety of antique pieces, which were chosen for their particular appeal rather than to create the mood of a particular historical period. One room has a tall antique armoire; two others have fireplaces; and three have king-size brass beds. Each room has a telephone and air conditioner and each either shares a balcony or has its own. A Continental breakfast is served in the dining room, and hors d'oeuvres are set out for evening get-togethers.

Accommodations: 4 rooms with shared bath. *Pets:* Not permitted. *Children:* Under twelve not permitted. *Driving Instructions:* Take I-45 into Galveston, where it becomes Broadway. Turn left on Seventeenth Street and drive five blocks to the inn.

THE NUTT HOUSE

Town Square, Granbury, TX 76048. 817-573-5612. *Innkeeper:* Madge Peters. Open all year.

The Nutt House has been offering Texas country cooking for many years. Now, to the joy of travelers, guest rooms on the second floor have been opened so that they can rise from the groaning board and go straight upstairs for a good night's sleep. Most of the rooms share bathrooms, but the nostalgia more than makes up for the short walk down the hall. Each of the rooms, which once were used by traveling salesmen, has hot and cold running water, ceiling fans, and quaint rattan mirrors. Old dressers and iron bedsteads add to the turn-of-the-century look.

The Nutt House was built in 1893 as a store operated by the Nutt family. Downstairs, in the dining rooms, guests and the public can sit down to a buffet meal. Dinner is served Tuesday through Friday from 11:30 to 2:00 and on weekends from 11:30 to 3:00. Supper is offered on Fridays and Saturdays only, from 6:00 to 8:00. The dining room serves regional foods of early Texas. In this region, this does not mean steak every day. The pioneers took foods familiar to them and added special touches unique to the Southwest. For instance, Mexican peppers were added to German sausage, and salt pork, a Southern dish, was frequently added to the traditional New England boiled dinner. The buffet always includes two entrées, four vegetables, salads, and home-baked breads and pies. Among the many regional specialties are chicken and dumplings, beef pot pie, meat loaf, and sliced ham — all served with grits and gravy. Accompanying these dishes are pots of beans, homemade chow chow, and tiny rounds of fried hot-water cornbread. Save room for dessert: hot peach cobbler or buttermilk pie.

Accommodations: 10 rooms, 1 with private bath, and 2 apartments. *Driving Instructions:* Take Route 377 southwest from Fort Worth.

Houston, Texas

LA COLOMBE D'OR

3410 Montrose Boulevard, Houston, TX 77006. 713-524-7999.
Innkeeper: Stephen N. Zimmerman. Open all year.

La Colombe d'Or is billed as "Houston's finest and only European chateau," paying homage to the famed *auberge* of the same name in St. Paul-de-Vence, France. Innkeeper Stephen Zimmerman has long admired the casual elegance and impeccable service of the French version, and he set out to create its counterpart in the United States.

The 21-room mansion was built in 1923 by Exxon's founder Walter Fondren for his family. It is set on landscaped grounds in the fashionable Montrose section of Houston, just minutes from the city's "magic circle" and the Galleria. Today the mansion offers French cuisine in attractive antique-filled dining rooms ensconced in the former music room and parlor. Wines, including ports and sherries, as well as traditional cocktails, are served in the library, which has the atmosphere of an English club. Upstairs are several lavish guest suites, each with museum-quality furnishings.

One suite, the Cézanne, is decorated in deep greens with rich tomato-colored accents. Its dining room overlooks the treetops and has a carved walnut table, chairs, and sideboard. The Renoir suite, a favorite, has a *Chinoise* theme with an antique carved headboard inlaid with ivory, lacquered chests, and a colorful cloisonné table. Visitors craving extra-special pampering can find no better place.

Accommodations: 5 suites with private bath. *Pets:* Not permitted. *Driving Instructions:* From I-45 take Main Street south to Westheimer Road. Turn right on Westheimer and then left on Montrose.

Jefferson, Texas

EXCELSIOR HOUSE

211 West Austin Street, Jefferson, TX 75657. 214-665-2513. Open all year.

Running the length of the front of Excelsior House is a gallery supported by ten iron posts, on top of which is a decorative iron railing. The hotel's Victorian ambience unfolds at the opening of its doors. In the golden days of Jefferson's past, the distinguished guest list included Ulysses S. Grant, Rutherford B. Hayes, Diamond Bessie, railroader Jay Gould, and Oscar Wilde. Today's Excelsior is no less fit to entertain presidents, thanks to the Jesse Allen Wise Garden Club, a group devoted to restoring historic Jefferson.

The hotel is a masterpiece of Southern restoration, with period antiques of maple, cherry, and mahogany all with the warmth and patina of age. Oriental rugs lie on richly colored wood floors, the pressed-tin and plaster ceilings are freshly painted, portraits cover the walls, and swagged drapes frame each window. Some of the furniture is of museum quality, such as the marble-topped Belter table in the ballroom or the flat-topped ceiling-height canopied bed (complete with tufted canopy cover). Equally distinctive are the sleigh and Jenny Lind spool beds in other guest rooms. The Excelsior is devoted to chandeliers, with a crystal one in the ballroom and an ornate brass and porcelain fixture from Dresden hanging in the dining room. Each of the guest rooms is special, with furnishings that complement its beds. In the morning, guests gather for a groaning-board Southern breakfast, the only meal served in the hotel.

The Excelsior is definitely worth the trip. Jefferson is a transition from the Texas bayous to its cattle country to the west and south. Texas is a big state, and the Excelsior is a fine place to rest up before pushing onward to see more.

Accommodations: 14 rooms and 1 suite with private bath. *Pets:* Not permitted. *Driving Instructions:* Take Route 59 to the center of Jefferson.

NEW JEFFERSON INN

124 West Austin Street, Jefferson, TX 75657. 214-665-2631.
Innkeepers: Mr. and Mrs. George Delk. Open all year.
In the 1850s and 1860s up to fifteen steamboats could be seen lined up at Jefferson's docks. Iron ore had been discovered nearby and a thriving pine, cypress, and cotton industry kept more than 30,000 persons financially secure in the town. Many tons of baled cotton were stored each year in the two-story brick warehouse on West Austin Street, which was built in 1861. And well built it was, with a laid-up-brick pyramid foundation that tapered from almost 8 feet at the base to the 18-inch walls of the warehouse itself. By 1900, the town's population had dwindled along with the river traffic because the railroad industry had bypassed Jefferson. That year, the warehouse was converted into a hotel. The Delks restored it in 1977, retaining many of the older features while adding such modernizations as acoustical ceilings and a textured "Spanish-tile" wall treatment.

The lobby of the hotel and many of the downstairs rooms have birch-paneled wainscoting. Also in the lobby are the original wicker couches and chairs. The guest rooms, most of which are on the top floor, have an old-fashioned look preserved through the use of antique brass, high-back Victorian and decorative iron beds, complemented by oak and marble-topped dressers, old rockers, and straight chairs. Other rooms have queen-size, newer brass beds but retain the older accessory furniture. Four of the bathrooms upstairs have claw-

foot tubs, while the others have more modern fixtures or showers. Some of the guest rooms still have the original ceiling fans.

The dining room at the New Jefferson offers breakfast and lunch Tuesday through Sunday, and dinners on Friday and Saturday only. The menu for all meals is à la carte, with a full "plantation" breakfast available. Luncheon specials often include Swiss steak, roast beef, baked ham, or chicken cacciatore on spaghetti. The weekend dinners include several steaks, a bacon-wrapped chopped sirloin, shrimp gumbo, fried shrimp, fried oysters, seafood platters, and boiled shrimp.

Accommodations: 22 rooms with private bath. *Driving Instructions:* Take Route 59 to the center of Jefferson.

PRIDE HOUSE

409 Broadway, Jefferson, TX 75657. 214-665-2675. *Innkeeper:* Ruthmary Jordan. Open all year.

The Pride House is a Victorian gingerbread guest house. There are stained-glass windows in every room, the original ornately decorated brass hardware on the five-paneled doors, and exceptional millwork and cabinetry throughout. The house was built by G. W. Brown, a sawmill owner, in 1889. He evidently used his finest hardwoods in the construction, and the three layers of thick wood wreaked havoc on the restorers' saws and drills. Fine woodwork can be seen in the beaded wainscoting, the moldings around the 9-foot windows, the transoms over the doors, and the trim in the rooms. The ceilings downstairs are 14 feet high, and those upstairs are not much lower. The feeling of the inn is quite Victorian, but as innkeeper Ruthmary Jordan is quick to point out, it is not a museum, and the furnishings are not limited to one period. One guest room is painted with a shutter-green enamel and has white woodwork and a red mantel over its working fireplace. The floor is red, and there is wicker furniture together with an old-fashioned iron-and-brass bed. Each guest room has a phone. Guests use antique armoires in the rooms in lieu of closets. For a morning treat, leave your blinds open when you retire: Sunlight shining through stained glass will brighten your day. Breakfast, which is set out in the old armoire in the upstairs hall, includes, in addition to typical Continental-breakfast items, such a special treat as hot gingerbread, tiny quiches, or poached pears.

The Pride House is painted a rich caramel color with spanking-white gingerbread trim. The side lawn is shaded by an old pecan tree. A front porch beckons guests with its antique rocking chairs and secluded old porch swing.

In addition to the rooms in the main house, there are two in a guest house called the Dependency, originally built for servants, which resembles a life-size dollhouse. Its kitchen is equipped with modern conveniences, and breakfast fixings are provided there. The house, which is rented as a unit, accommodates up to seven guests. A porch swing adds a romantic touch.

Accommodations: 4 rooms with private bath in the Pride House and 2 rooms in the Dependency. *Pets and children:* Permitted in the Dependency only. *Driving Instructions:* From the junction with Highway 59 in Jefferson, take Highway 49 (Broadway) east 3 blocks.

WISE MANOR

312 Houston Street, Jefferson, TX 75657. 214-665-2386. *Innkeeper:* Katherine Ramsay Wise. Open all year.

Wise Manor is a gem of a Victorian home. Looking as if it has just stepped out of a fairy tale, the little two-story cottage is painted in salmon tones with crisp, white gingerbread trim. Surrounded by large pecan trees, it peers out from behind a wrought-iron fence in the older section of town. Innkeeper Katherine Wise has furnished the house with Victorian pieces from three generations of her family. The look of the place is fresh and clean, with ruffleu curtains at the windows and marble-topped tables adorned with fresh seasonal flowers in the guest rooms. Antique white bedspreads and folded appliquéd quilts cover ornate walnut beds. A Continental breakfast is served, although Mrs. Wise will arrange for a plantation breakfast at the nearby Excelsior House if desired.

Accommodations: 3 rooms with private bath. *Pets:* Not permitted. *Driving Instructions:* From the junction of I-20 and U.S. 59 drive north through Marshall and continue 17 miles to Jefferson.

THE BADU HOUSE

601 Bessemer, Llano, TX 78643. 915-247-4304. *Innkeeper:* Ann Ruff. Open all year except Christmas and the first two weeks in January.

Llano is a ranching town in the Texas hill country. One of its earliest buildings was the First National Bank, built in Italian Renaissance style in 1891. In 1898 Professor Badu and his wife, Charlie Neal Badu, bought the bank and made it into their home. The Badu family lived there until the late 1970s, when they sold the building to Ann and Earl Ruff. The sturdy structure, in fine shape but in need of some tender loving care and elbow grease, was transformed over the next few years into a fanciful country inn. The restoration was done under the expert guidance of Ann Ruff, the Lone Star State's leading authority on Texas country inns, who researched and wrote a number of guidebooks.

The Badu House is listed in the National Register of Historic Places. Among its notable features are unusual shutters and bronze and brass hardware, all original to the building. The flower motif on the window pulls, doorknobs, hinges, and so forth, is now the Badu House logotype; and there is a stained-glass window at the head of the stairs. The upstairs guest rooms, which have paneling brought from England, are furnished in a variety of antiques including family heirlooms. The largest room, Aberdeen, contains Eastlake Victorian pieces originally belonging to Ann's great-grandmother. The baths all have claw-footed tubs, pedestal sinks, and pull-chain commodes.

The bar and several intimate dining rooms downstairs are also decorated with antiques. The Badu House's pride and joy, the bar, is covered by a rare mineral, llanite, which was discovered by Professor Badu and is found only in Llano County.

Lunch and dinner are served to the public, with Ann cooking up such specialties as green chili soup, fried corn bread crepes, fried fruit pies, and Mississippi corn-fed catfish.

Accommodations: 8 rooms, 6 with private bath. *Pets and children:* Not permitted. *Driving Instructions:* The inn is at the intersection of Routes 71, 16, and 29.

THE CASTLE

1403 E. Washington, Navasota, TX 77868. 409-825-8051. *Innkeepers:* Helen and Tim Urquhart. Open all year.

The Castle is a Victorian fantasy that includes yellow brick walls, a copper-roofed tower, 14-foot-high medallioned ceilings, elaborate woodwork and parquet floors, and beveled and stained glass windows. Built in 1893, it remained in one family until 1956 and escaped many so-called "improvements." The innkeepers, Tim and Helen Urquhart, have filled the rooms with a collection of Victorian antiques. The entrance door sparkles with 100 beveled panes of glass, and one need only pass through the portal to be transported back to the turn of the century. The glow of a twenty-foot-high stained glass window lights the landing of the heavily carved spindle staircase. Upstairs are the guest rooms and an authentically decorated sitting balcony where a Continental breakfast is served. The tower sitting room is a favorite spot for reading or visiting fellow guests. The four guest rooms are furnished with marble-topped bureaus and washstands, Oriental rugs, and an unusual bed. One room, for example, has a Louisiana plantation bed, and another, a walnut half-tester. Two of the inn's fireplaces are in guest rooms.

Accommodations: 4 room with private bath. *Pets and children under 14:* Not permitted. *Driving Instructions:* From Houston take Route 290 to Hempstead, then Route 6 to Navasota and Route 105 (Washington Avenue). From Bryan take Route 6 south to Route 105 and turn right.

FAUST HOTEL

240 South Seguin Avenue, New Braunfels, TX 78130. 512-625-7791. *Innkeeper:* Gary R. Cattell. Open all year.

The Faust Hotel underwent extensive restoration in 1982. The brick and carved stonework of the exterior were cleaned, and the interior was polished, painted, and redecorated. The four-story hotel, built in 1928, had been a fashionable dining and overnight stop in the very heart of historic New Braunfels, and it retains the glamour of fifty years ago. The innkeeper reupholstered the overstuffed chairs and couches, dusted off the lighting fixtures, and cleaned and oiled the old-fashioned ceiling paddle fans that cool almost all the rooms, including the guest rooms. The fans are augmented by air conditioning, and there is cable color television in each guest room. The ambience is that of the 1920s and 1930s.

Guest rooms are individually decorated with comfortable furnishings, heavy armoires, and candlestick telephones. Each has original furniture, fixtures, patterned carpets, pictures, and memorabilia. Every room has its original bathroom, with little ceramic tiles, the old porcelain fixtures, and claw-footed tub. The one suite has a sitting room with a bar and comfortable club chairs around a sturdy antique table.

Downstairs the old lobby clock still ticks away on the wall. The tile-floored lobby-lounge is filled with old pieces and tropical plants and potted trees. The barroom boasts paddle fans and lacy, old-fashioned curtains at the tall windows.

The dining room re-creates the era with its napkins, cloths, green plants, and decorative screens and the dark woods of the bentwood chairs. The public and guests are offered country-style breakfasts, luncheons, and dinners by a bar- and dining-room staff that dresses in 1920s uniforms. Room service is available.

Accommodations: 62 rooms with private bath. *Pets:* Not permitted. *Driving Instructions:* New Braunfels is 35 miles northeast of San Antonio, off I-35 just north of the highway. The hotel is three blocks from the scenic Comal River and half a block from the town square.

PRINCE SOLMS INN

295 East San Antonio Street, New Braunfels, TX 78130. 512-625-9169. *Innkeeper:* Ruth L. Wood. Open all year.

New Braunfels, founded in 1845 by a German prince, Carl Solms-Braunfels, retains much of its German heritage. People flock from all over to celebrate Wurtsfest — a week-long festival of Bavarian dancing and feasting in late October. A popular tourist attraction, this historic town has been called "The Sausage Capital of Texas," "The Antiquing Capital of Texas," and "The Beauty Spot of Texas."

In the heart of town is the Prince Solms Inn. Built in 1900, it has spent most of its existence welcoming guests. The handsome Victorian structure is a tribute to the craftsmanship of its German builders. In recent years, the inn has been restored and many antique fixtures and accessories have been added that enhance its period decor. Carriage lights flanking the tall entranceway came from a manor house in Texas; solid bronze doorknobs and hinges, from an aging Chicago mansion; and the ceiling fans with their antique lighting fixtures, from an early San Antonio building.

The Prince Solms's guest parlor and bedrooms are furnished with Victorian antiques. The inn exemplifies the area's historic past, and unobtrusive tours are offered to the public each afternoon. The Prince Solms Inn has made a few concessions to modern-day comfort, with air conditioning and heating. The lone television set is hidden in an antique linen press in the parlor. A buffet breakfast is set out in the hall, and guests may take the food to their rooms, which contain breakfast areas.

The inn's restaurant and turn-of-the-century lounge-bar are in its basement, with 30-inch-thick stone walls and floor of polished brown concrete that appears to be made of leather. The restaurant, Wolfgang's Keller, features steaks, chicken, and veal specialties, accompanied by light sauces and brown rice.

One block from the inn is Landa Park and the crystal-clear spring-fed Comal River. Here, guests can bike, swim, golf, and enjoy boating in a scenic setting. At the nearby Guadalupe River, canoeing, rafting, and tubing are popular pastimes. River Road follows the Guadalupe beside its white-water rapids, cypress trees, and 200-foot-high cliffs. The river ends below the Canyon Lake Dam, an 8,000-acre lake.

Accommodations: 10 rooms with private bath. *Pets and children:* Not permitted. *Driving Instructions:* New Braunfels is just north of San Antonio, on I-35.

LA BORDE HOUSE

601 East Main Street, Rio Grande, TX 78582. 512-487-5101. *Innkeeper:* Maria L. Sanchez. Open all year.

François La Borde commissioned Parisian architects to design his home, which is just a block from the Rio Grande River. Over the years, La Borde House acquired various additions and served for much of that time as a travelers' way station. Early guests included those traveling to Texas political events, riverboat travelers, and cattle barons who sold their herds on nearby river docks.

The hotel was purchased recently by the Sheerin family of San Antonio, who sponsored its restoration with the guidance of the Texas Historical Commission and the U.S. Department of the Interior. The thorough restoration included reconstructing all the inn's windows, recarving many of the wooden stair balusters, and hand-cutting many replacement pieces of gingerbread trim. The decorative iron gate was rebuilt to look as it did in 1898, giving the entrance to La Borde House a look reminiscent of New Orleans. The hotel is constructed largely of brick, and replacements were obtained from the same Carmargo, Mexico, brickyard where the original bricks were cast.

The hotel's furniture was collected throughout the South and West and is typical of the period, and there are Oriental rugs and English Axminster carpets throughout. Each bedroom bears a name commemorating a bit of local history. Many of the papers and fabrics are the same as those used during the recent restoration of the Texas Governor's Mansion. In one guest room a massive carved half-tester Victorian bed is cooled by the slowly turning blades of an illuminated ceiling fan. A caned rocker in another room sits beside a bed backed by an antique bookcase filled with century-old bound volumes. In a third room a high-back bed has 7-foot posts rising to a pleated full canopy. Along with the authentic rooms and their furnishings there are modern amenities, including full baths, many with pull-chain toilets, clawfooted bathtubs, pedestal sinks, and tile floors. Eight-channel television is available in all guest rooms and a wide selection of movies is available for showing in the parlor, with advance notice. Guests may relax in the parlor and library, as well as in a tropical courtyard.

Accommodations: 8 restored guest rooms with private bath, plus 13 one-room efficiency apartments. *Pets:* Not permitted. *Driving Instructions:* Take Route 83 to Rio Grande City.

San Antonio, Texas

MENGER HOTEL AND MOTOR INN

204 Alamo Plaza, San Antonio, TX 78205. 512-223-4361; toll-free from out of state: 800-327-9157. Open all year.

The Menger Hotel has had as colorful a history as that of the old West it served. The hotel was built in 1859 — just twenty-three years after the fall of the Alamo, which stands alongside the Menger — by a German brewer, William Menger, to provide elegant lodgings for patrons of his brewery, the first in Texas. Facing the Alamo Plaza, the hotel was the scene of many an antebellum ball. Later, Teddy Roosevelt recruited his Rough Riders at the bar — a replica of the bar in the House of Lords in London — where untold numbers of cattle deals were sealed over a handshake and a shot of whiskey. The Menger has been host to five U.S. presidents and many other notables from far and wide, including Generals Lee and Grant and stars of stage and screen.

Today the historic hotel, although greatly enlarged, is as elegant as ever. The newer lobby-lounge has a glass wall looking out into the gardens, where a swimming pool is shaded by tall palms. Marble floors are covered with thick carpets. In the oldest section, the open rotunda is lighted by a skylight set three stories above the lobby. Antiques and oil paintings of the old West decorate the halls. Guest rooms open onto the two stories of balconies in this section and are furnished with Victorian antiques blended with more traditional hotel furnishings. The 225 rooms in the new sections are more modern. The Roy Rogers Room, where Roy and his wife, Dale Evans, stayed during their moviemaking days, is furnished in rawhide and leather. The Devon Suite, which has a small sitting room, is furnished with heavy carved antiques, including a canopied bed. The wallpaper here has a bold floral design on a dark background. The King Suite has a spacious parlor, antique furnishings, and a four-poster bed. Its balcony overlooks the plaza. Downstairs are several public rooms, including a coffee shop and a formal dining room with crystal chandeliers and wine-red carpeting. Both are open to the public for all meals.

Accommodations: 325 rooms with private bath. *Driving Instructions:* In San Antonio take Commerce Street to North Alamo Street. Turn north and proceed to Alamo Plaza and the hotel.

San Marcos, Texas

AQUARENA SPRINGS INN

Aquarena Drive, San Marcos, Texas. Mailing address: P.O. Box 2330, San Marcos, TX 78666. 512-396-8901. *Innkeeper:* Al McGehee. Open all year.

This inn is in the center of the Aquarena Springs family amusement area. Built in 1929, the former resort hotel was often the locale of rooftop dances featuring big-name bands of that era. The inn was closed during the Depression and equipped as a hospital and health spa. It was later leased to a school for exceptional children, was remodeled in 1961, and reopened as the resort hotel for Aquarena Springs. Each room has been refurbished in a modern style. Throughout the building, the original high ceilings have been retained to maintain a spacious, old-fashioned feeling. Nineteen of the guest rooms have balconies overlooking the clear, spring-fed San Marcos River and the cypress trees lining its banks. The other six rooms overlook a moss-covered cliff. Guests of the Inn have access to nature trails in the Hanging Gardens on the cliff above the inn, as well as the Olympic-size swimming pool and the Aquarena Springs Golf Course, which adjoin the inn. The Aquarena Springs Restaurant is nearby.

Accommodations: 25 rooms with private bath. *Pets:* Not permitted. *Driving Instructions:* Follow I-35 to San Marcos. Take the Aquarena Springs exit and follow the signs to Aquarena Springs.

VON MINDEN HOTEL

607 Lyons Street, Schulenburg, TX 78956. 409-743-3493. *Innkeepers:* Bill and Betty Pettit. Open all year.

The Von Minden Hotel seems to exist in the 1930s or 1940s. Guests walking into the lobby would have no way of knowing they were in the second half of the twentieth century. Little has changed. Overstuffed chairs and couches are grouped together. Old radios are set on shelves, a dark wood-paneled phone booth stands next to the front desk, and a tiny antique shop is tucked into a corner by the stairs. Likewise, the guest rooms have changed little. If one wants to know what it was like to stay in an old salesman's hotel, this is it.

A half century ago it was a common practice for rural Texas hotels to also house a movie theater. Now the Von Minden's Cozy Theater is the last one of its kind in the state. As one walks down the second-floor hallway in the evening, the clicking of the ancient movie projector can be heard.

The guest rooms are furnished with sturdy mission-style furniture made by the men who built the hotel. The bathrooms have the original fixtures, including enameled tin tubs. The iron beds are set on braided rugs, and a Gideon Bible rests on each bedside table. Although the hotel is almost exactly as it was in earlier days, it is tidy and clean. With a bow to modern comfort, the rooms are air-conditioned (in case the paddle fans can't do the job), and color television sets have been installed. On the third floor, the Hard Times Restaurant and Bar offers steaks and seafood nightly to guests and the public.

Accommodations: 40 rooms, 20 with private bath. *Pets:* Not permitted. *Driving Instructions:* From I-10 take the Schulenburg exit south to the town. The inn is on Lyons Street, one block south of Main Street.

Weimar, Texas

WEIMAR COUNTRY INN

101 Jackson Street, Weimar, Texas. Mailing address: P.O. Box 782, Weimar, TX 78962. 409-725-8888. *Innkeeper:* Laura Smith. Open all year.

The town of Weimar was founded in the 1870s when construction of the G. H. & S. A. Railroad crossed the Colorado River and headed toward San Antonio. Among those who let the tracks cross their land were Mr. Borden, the inventor of canned milk, and Mr. Jackson, on whose land the railroad depot would be built and around which Weimar would grow.

The Jackson Hotel, built to accommodate rail travelers, burned in 1909 and was rebuilt on the same spot. In 1981 the hotel was bought by a group of investors, restored, and renovated. Today it is a small inn furnished with country-Victorian antiques set off by polished floors and old-fashioned wallpapers. The dining room serves family-style meals Thursday through Saturday, with steaks, including the Texas fried steaks, as the house specialty.

A Continental breakfast is set out in the sitting room upstairs. The guest rooms have stained-glass transoms, lace curtains, antiques, and hand-made quilts that reflect the soft colors of the floral wallpapers. The ceiling fans are augmented by air conditioning.

Accommodations: 9 rooms, 7 with private bath. *Pets:* Not permitted. *Driving Instructions:* Take Route 155 off I-10 and drive to Route 90. Turn left and go to the second light. Turn left again, and cross the tracks to Jackson and Center streets.

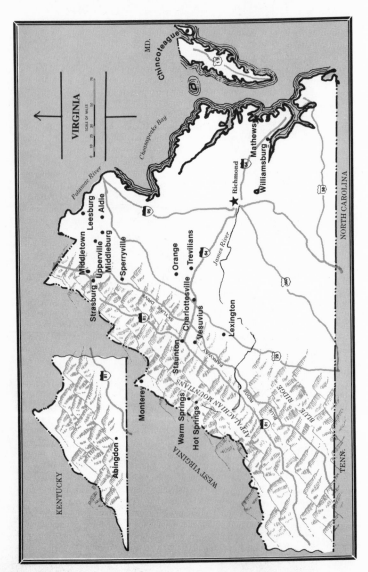

Virginia

Abingdon, Virginia

The resort town of Abingdon, just above the Tennessee border in the Virginia Highlands, is the seat of Washington County and the center of Virginia's burley tobacco market. There is a *Burley Tobacco Festival* the first weekend of every October, and in the first two weeks of August, the county celebrates with the *Virginia Highlands Festival.* Tourists and native Virginians flock to Abingdon to hear the Highlands musical entertainments see plays, and browse among the rustic-crafts exhibits and demonstrations. The most famous attraction in town is the historic *Barter Theater*, across from the Martha Washington Inn on Main Street. The theater is now the State Theater of Virginia, performing a wide range of plays and offering a special children's theater as well. Performances run from April through October, and the children's show is from the middle of June through August. For information, call 703-628-3991.

THE MARTHA WASHINGTON INN
150 West Main Street, Abingdon, VA 24210. 703-628-3161.
Innkeeper: Ellison Ketchum. Open all year.
The Martha Washington Inn is a historic beauty that has recently been the object of a costly and comprehensive restoration. The grand old Southern lady was purchased by a group of dedicated Virginia businessmen bent on preserving her in a manner befitting her age and station in the community. More than $750,000 was spent for polishing,

painting, refurbishing, and restoring. The grounds were landscaped to provide her with a properly elegant setting. The interior, with its gracious broad hall and fine parlors, harbors many of the antiques originally in the house. A particularly fine grandfather clock still keeps time from its station in the front lobby, shaded by a colonnaded veranda. Some of the most impressive furniture resides in the guest rooms, where guests may spend their nights under the high canopy of an elaborately carved bed in one room or in Victorian splendor in another. Some of the rooms have working fireplaces. There are many antiques throughout the inn, in the public rooms and dining rooms as well as in the guest rooms.

The Martha Washington Inn began in 1832 as the private home of Patrick Henry's niece and her husband, General Francis Preston. In 1854 it became a Methodist women's college, which operated through the Civil War. The romance of this period has led to many stories concerning wounded soldiers and the college girls, secret staircases, floors with unremovable bloodstains, and phantom horses. The best known of these eerie tales concerns a mortally wounded Yankee soldier's being nursed by a Southern girl: She played her violin softly to him each evening to comfort him. His death broke her heart, and today some say one can still hear the strains of a ghostly violin around midnight on certain evenings.

The Cameo Room, the inn's restaurant, offers a selection of traditional Southern favorites, as well as Continental cuisine such as duckling with cognac, filet mignon stuffed with fresh oysters and wrapped with bacon, and poulet des pommes — boned chicken breast stuffed with apple and walnuts and topped with a light brandied cream sauce. If you wish to explore the area, including some of Virginia's highest mountains, the inn will pack you a picnic basket of goodies and send you off with a helpful map.

On warm, pleasant afternoons the old-fashioned rocking chairs on the inn's front porch are filled with guests taking the fresh air and enjoying the complimentary afternoon tea service. From May through October the historic Barter Theatre across the street (affiliated with the State Theatre of Virginia) offers a variety of plays for children or for adults.

Accommodations: 80 rooms with private bath. *Pets:* Not permitted. *Driving Instructions:* Take exit 8 off I-81. The inn is in the heart of Abingdon.

Aldie, Virginia

LITTLE RIVER INN

U.S. 50, Aldie, Virginia. Mailing address: P.O. Box 116, Aldie, VA 22001. 703-327-6742. *Innkeeper:* Barbara Weir. Open all year.

The Little River Inn is a country house of painted brick with wavy tiny-paned windows flanked by dark shutters. Evidence of the loving care this old house receives is in its trim border gardens, which skirt the veranda and back patio. Crisp ruffled curtains at the windows; pine, cherry, and walnut antique furnishings; and fires in the hearths add to the welcoming atmosphere.

Reconstructed in 1868 using the brick walls of an 1810 house, the building was completely restored in 1982, opening as an inn that same year. The guest rooms are decorated with antiques and early quilts. Some rooms have hand-stenciled borders, and one has a fireplace in its sitting area. In 1983, an adjacent log cabin and eighteenth-century Patent House were also restored. Each has a sitting room with a fireplace and wide-plank floors. A full complimentary breakfast is served here or in the main house. The Little River Inn is just 35 miles from Washington, D.C., in the heart of Virginia's hunt country. Middleburg and Leesburg are nearby, with shops, restaurants, and historic sites.

Accommodations: 5 rooms, 2 with private bath, and 2 cottages. *Pets:* Not permitted. *Children:* Under 10 not permitted. *Driving Instructions:* From Washington, D.C., drive west on I-66 to the U.S. 50 exit. Continue west on U.S. 50 for 16 miles.

Charlottesville, Virginia

SILVER THATCH INN

3001 Hollymead Drive, Charlottesville, VA 22901. 804-978-4686. *Innkeepers:* Tim and Shelley Dwight. Open all year except the last two weeks in January.

Silver Thatch Inn is a Colonial building with a long and interesting history. The first section was built in 1780 by Hessian soldiers captured at the Battle of Saratoga in New York, who were marched to Charlottesville and instructed to build their own barracks. In 1801 the building was enlarged and converted to a boys' school. Later it saw service as a tavern and coach stop and, still later, as a private plantation. In the 1930s, with another addition, it became the home of a dean at the University of Virginia.

Tim and Shelley Dwight purchased the sprawling white clapboard building in 1984 and have since transformed it into an attractive inn, once again offering food and lodging to travelers. The inn is furnished with antique beds, dressers, and armoires accented by country-style quilts. With a bow to modern amenities, there are tennis courts and a swimming pool on the landscaped grounds. The three "country formal" dining rooms feature French cuisine served by candlelight. Five entrées are prepared nightly by chef-innkeeper, Shelley Dwight.

Accommodations: 5 rooms with private bath. *Pets:* Not permitted. *Driving Instructions:* From Charlottesville, take Route 29 north 8 miles to the inn.

Chincoteague, Virginia

THE CHANNEL BASS INN

100 Church Street, Chincoteague, VA 23336. 804-336-6148.
Innkeeper: James S. Hanretta. Open all year except January and December. Restaurant closed Monday and Tuesday.

The exterior of the Channel Bass Inn gives no real hint of the pleasures awaiting inside its doors. This island house grew up as the need arose after it was built in the 1860s. Over the years, a third floor with lots of dormers was added, as well as a glassed-in porch complete with such modern touches as asbestos shingle on the walls and asphalt shingle on the roof. But guests who venture inside will find a unique gastronomic experience.

Jim Hanretta, the owner-chef, trained in Spain and France. Dinners here reflect Jim's respect for food, his affection for Spanish culture and the Basque countryside, and his reliance on the sea's bountiful provisions. Five choices of seafood appetizers include oysters Basque (with parmesan cheese, chorizo sausage, and tomato sauce), oysters continental (in a tarragon wine sauce), and steamed Chincoteague clams. Specialties included in eleven entrées are seafood espagnol (shrimp, lobster, oyster, clams, scallops, chorizo sausage, and bacon in sauce espagnol), and trois de mer (shrimp, scallops, and lobster sautéed in white wine, butter, and garlic). There are also additional seafood dishes, beef dishes, and a special rice dish that is an aromatic blend of saffron, rice, pepper, onion, tomato, chicken stock, and chorizo sausage.

The inn's guest rooms vary in both size and furnishings. The third floor has been restored, and the second floor is mostly original. All rooms are furnished simply — with antiques, others with reproductions. Original artwork hangs on the walls, watercolors and pen-and-ink renderings of the island's birds and other wildlife. Six of the guest rooms have either king- or queen-size beds. Each room is individually air-conditioned and heated.

The innkeeper offers cooking seminars in the off season: Rates over three days include lodging, meals, and three four-hour seminars.

Accommodations: 10 rooms with private bath. *Pets:* Not permitted. *Children:* Under eleven not permitted. *Driving Instructions:* From Salisbury, Maryland, take Route 13 south approximately 40 miles to Route 175, and then to Chincoteague. When Route 175 becomes a dead end on Main Street, turn left, go two blocks to Church Street, and turn right. The inn is the first house on the right.

MISS MOLLY'S INN

113 North Main Street, Chincoteague, VA 23336. 804-336-6686. *Innkeepers:* Dr. and Mrs. James C. Stam. Open April through November.

Chincoteague is an unspoiled island, famous for its wild ponies, oysters, and clam shoals. The windswept beauty of nearby Assateague National Seashore and Chincoteague National Wildlife Refuge are minutes away. This inn, an ideal base for enjoying all that the islands and little fishing village have to offer, is a large Queen Anne–style Victorian just 150 feet from the shore and docking oyster boats. It was built in 1886 by Mr. Rowley. His daughter Molly lived in the house for eighty-four years and was one of the island's best-loved citizens. How could the inn be called anything but Miss Molly's?

Most schoolchildren know Chincoteague and its ponies from the novel *Misty of Chincoteague.* Its author, Marguerite Henry, wrote the book while a guest at Miss Molly's.

Four porches offer views of spectacular sunsets over the water, and there are gazebos and picket fences set off by pink and red roses. The 25-room house is furnished with turn-of-the-century antiques and comfortable overstuffed chairs. A portrait of Miss Molly hangs in the stairwell. The innkeepers, Jim and Priscilla, restored the inn, papering the rooms with flowered and striped wallpapers and putting lace curtains on the windows. The Stams serve a full breakfast and afternoon tea to overnight guests.

Accommodations: 7 rooms, 1 with private bath. *Pets:* Not permitted. *Children:* Under twelve not permitted. *Driving Instructions:* From Salisbury, Maryland, take Route 13 south to Route 175 and then drive eastward. At Chincoteague Island, turn left on Main Street and drive 2½ blocks to the inn.

Hot Springs, Virginia

THE HOMESTEAD

Route 220, Hot Springs, VA 24445. 703-839-5500. Open all year. More than three centuries ago, an American Indian brave discovered warm mineral water bubbling out of a fissure in the earth amid what are now known as the Blue Ridge Mountains of Virginia. Almost without a pause since the mid-seventeenth century, guests seeking the healthful waters have been drawn to the towns of Hot Springs and

Warm Springs. The Homestead in Hot Springs is a very special Southern resort that has offered an unbroken tradition of pampering its guests with almost any imaginable service and fine food since the first hotel was built on its grounds in 1891. The tone of our visit was established the moment we stepped through the Homestead's doors into its Great Hall. The strains of a string ensemble playing for guests at teatime greeted us, and we were instantly transported to another era.

This is no quaint little inn. There seem to be miles of corridors at The Homestead. Its guest rooms and parlors accommodate 1,100 guests, and the staff in attendance always exceeds the number of people registered. Guests may choose between a recently constructed ultramodern hotel wing and the more traditional rooms in the earlier section that we prefer. There, the decor and furnishings are reminiscent of a fine European hotel, and the service blends European traditions with Southern hospitality. The arrangement of much of The Homestead is of bedrooms separated by parlor rooms. Thus there is the choice of renting one room, or several suite combinations. For the kind of splurge that the Homestead is likely to be, we recommend adding the small charge for a parlor room.

Included in the daily rate at the Homestead are the rooms, three full meals, use of the indoor pool, a nightly movie, dancing, and afternoon tea. For additional charges one may enjoy bowling, carriage rides, golfing on three eighteen-hole courses, ice-skating, skiing on the Homestead slopes within walking distance of the hotel, tennis, and spa facilities including mineral baths, massage, steam room, and sauna.

For us, all of these recreational facilities took a backseat to what must be described as the Homestead's awesome parade of food from dawn to dusk. We stopped trying to count the hot and cold dishes on the breakfast buffet, but have it on good authority that the luncheon offerings usually reach 150 items. At dinner an elegant à la carte menu, different each day, offers up to a dozen special entrées. The Continental cuisine offered at the Homestead is prepared by a staff of sixty-five cooks, bakers, and pastry men and served in the dining room by a veritable army of highly trained waiters. The Homestead's traditions date back more than a century; it is certainly a very special place.

Accommodations: 600 rooms. *Driving Instructions:* Ask for the Homestead's brochure detailing the best routes.

VINE COTTAGE INN

Route 220, Hot Springs, Virginia. Mailing address: P.O. Box 205, Hot Springs, VA 24445. 703-839-2422. *Innkeeper*: Wendell Lucas. Open all year.

The Vine Cottage Inn is just 500 yards from the famed "country spa" the Homestead, in the Warm Springs Mountains of the Alleghenies. The cottage was built in 1903 as an annex to the historic hotel by its owners, the Virginia Hot Springs Inc. The inn's wide veranda is lined with white-wicker rockers. Flowers, shrubbery, and the forested mountains are the backdrop for the big turn-of-the-century house with its many-angled gables and wraparound porch. Its innkeepers purchased the inn lock, stock, and barrel from the previous owners, who had spent years restoring, refinishing, and adding an eclectic collection of antiques. Three of the larger guest rooms are dorms that sleep up to six people each and are popular with hunting, fishing, and skiing groups, and with large families. On the inn's ground floor is a suite with a private entrance off a secluded side porch. A kitchen, a sitting room complete with overstuffed couch, chairs, and television, and two double bedrooms are all part of the unit, which is accented with Victorian antiques. The other guest rooms are individually decorated. One has been modernized with walnut paneling and a shower bath, but for the most part the rooms have the old-fashioned look and feel of the early 1900s. There is a sink in each room, and ten of the rooms have private baths with claw-footed tubs. Other individual baths are down the hall, as they were in Grandma's day. Many of the beds are covered with the original "Vine Cottage" embroidered spreads.

The inn's spacious living room invites guests to relax and chat with fellow lodgers or to curl up by the fire with a book from the walnut bookcases. The room's dark walnut wainscoting contrasts sharply with the beige plaster walls. The mantel of the brick hearth is also walnut, setting off the ornately framed Constable print.

The Vine Cottage Inn is popular in all four seasons, with cross-country and downhill skiing at the Homestead nearby, trout fishing in national-forest brooks in the spring, hiking in the summer, and spectacular foliage and hunting every autumn. A complimentary breakfast is served.

Accommodations: 17 rooms, 10 with private bath. *Driving Instructions:* The inn is next to the Homestead on Route 220, within the town limits of Hot Springs, 5 miles south of Warm Springs.

Leesburg, Virginia

LAUREL BRIGADE INN

20 West Market Street, Leesburg, VA 22075. 703-777-1010. *Innkeeper*: Ellen Flippo Wall. Open mid-February through December. The Laurel Brigade Inn is a handsome 1759 structure of cut-and-fitted native Virginia stone. Its entranceway is framed by a rare ivy that spreads up one corner and across the lobby's side porch. The innkeeper, Ellen Wall, is constantly asked for cuttings. Guests enter the inn through the lobby, which doubles as a sitting room and is furnished with antiques and appropriate reproductions. There are delicate "lady's chairs," a Chippendale sofa, and an enormous table of rare black Italian marble that many visitors say is quite valuable and that Ellen claims was left by the previous owners because it was too heavy to move. Five guest rooms with spacious private baths are available to overnight guests. Each is decorated with quilt-covered canopied bedsteads and a combination of period antiques and suitable reproductions, which are handcrafted by Clore, a group of fifth-generation German cabinetmakers who fashion pieces without using glue or nails.

The Laurel Brigade's meals attract hungry Washingtonians to Leesburg. The dining rooms vary in size and atmosphere from the hundred-seat main dining room, which opens through French doors onto enclosed gardens, to snug cubbyholes. Meals feature simple, plentiful dishes at reasonable prices. House specialties include such fresh seafood dishes as Laurel crab cakes and flounder stuffed with crabmeat, and country-fried chicken, Virginia ham, and steaks. Three fresh vegetables are passed family-style at the evening meals and Sundays, and there are baskets of hot rolls on the tables. The inn is famous for its home-baked pastries, and in a vote on favorites, apple pie would probably win hands down. The restaurant is open from noon to 2 for lunch and 5 to 8 for dinner. Sunday meals run from noon to 7, and the restaurant is closed Monday.

Accommodations: 5 rooms with private bath. *Driving Instructions:* Leesburg is on Route 7, and the inn is in the center of town, half a block west off U.S. 15.

THE NORRIS HOUSE INN

108 Louden Street, S.W., Leesburg, Virginia. Mailing address: P.O. Box 966, Leesburg, VA 22075. 703-777-1806. *Innkeepers:* Amy and Craig DeRemer. Open all year.

The Norris House Inn was built in 1806 on a narrow side street in historic Leesburg, just one hour from Washington, D.C. A worn brick sidewalk runs past the inn's brick-enclosed side yard, with its tall pines, magnolia tree, flower gardens, and decorative antique sleigh. In warm weather red geraniums add bright color to the orange brick building, with its dark green shutters and sturdy double front door.

Just above this entryway a glassed-in sitting room juts out. Downstairs there is an inviting parlor on either side of the hall. The original interior shutters are still at all the windows, which have old wavy glass in their tiny twelve-over-twelve panes. One of the two parlors is decorated in blues and whites, with a blue-and-white sofa facing an ornate fireplace and an old-fashioned Victrola standing in the corner. The other contains formal Victorian pieces, including an oak settee and an antique parlor organ. Old oil paintings add to its appeal. Local craftsmen frequently display their work in the public rooms. The dining room's trim is accented in Victorian fashion with cinnamon and coffee colors above walnut wainscoting. A large pewter chandelier lights the polished antique table, with its bouquet of fresh flowers. A

built-in walnut hutch holds a silver tea service. It is here that breakfast is served. The morning meal usually includes several specialties, such as lemon muffins, fried apples, or salmon quiche.

Each guest room is furnished with antiques, and two have working fireplaces. Antique quilts, many from the families of the innkeepers, top guest room beds, including a queen-size four-poster in one room. Personal touches at Norris House include complimentary port and sherry in the evening and chocolates made especially for the inn, which are left on guests' pillows at night.

Accommodations: 4 rooms with shared bath. *Pets:* Not permitted. *Children:* Young children not encouraged. *Driving Instructions:* From Washington, D.C., take Route 7 into Leesburg. Keep left at the fork and then drive four blocks to the inn, which will be on your left.

Lexington, Virginia

Lexington, a historic town of 7,500 in western Virginia near the West Virginia border, contains many lovely restored buildings and is the home of Virginia Military Institute and Washington and Lee University, both of which have lovely campuses with handsome buildings. The best way to see historic Lexington is to take the walking tour starting at the Visitor's Information Center, which is housed in a century-old brick building at 107 East Washington Street. Parking is available nearby, and the center offers pamphlets about area attractions and a map of a walking tour.

Lexington is steeped in the tradition of two great Civil War generals, Stonewall Jackson and Robert E. Lee, both of whom lived here. The *Stonewall Jackson House* at East Washington Street was the only home the general ever owned. The life of Jackson in his Lexington days is portrayed by exhibits and described by an interpretative staff. Admission is charged. The *Lee Chapel* is considered the town's leading attraction. Built during the general's presidency of Washington College, the chapel contains the Lee crypt and the Washington and Lee Museum, with its collection of famous paintings. The chapel is open daily without charge. *Washington Hall*, an 1824 neoclassical brick building, bears a wooden statue of Washington. The building was built by Colonel John Jordan and formed the basis of the emerging campus that was to become one of the most beautiful in the country. The *President's House*, the home of the university president, was designed by Lee for his own use. The *Lee-Jackson House* (1842) is the spot where Jackson married his wife, Elinor. It is currently an administrative building for the university. The *Robert E. Lee Memorial Episcopal Church* was built just after the general's death. The *Lexington Presbyterian Church* was built in 1843; here, Jackson founded and taught a Sunday-school class for the black members of the congregation.

THE ALEXANDER-WITHROW HOUSE

3 West Washington Street, Lexington, VA 24450. 703-463-2044. *Innkeeper*: Don Fredenburg. Open all year.

The Alexander-Withrow House, built in 1789, is a house of firsts in Lexington. In the past, it served as the first school, the first post office, the first bank, and as several stores. Thomas J. (Stonewall) Jackson served on the board of directors at the time the building was used as the bank. The house is somewhat unusual in that its first floor is built of stone and its two upper floors of brick. The diamond patterns formed by the use of glazed brick are the most striking feature of the exterior. A wrought-iron balcony extends across part of the building at the second-floor level, and there is a chimney in each of the four corners of the house.

Upstairs, on four floors, are the guest suites. These generally have a living room with double hide-a-bed, a bedroom with double bed, and a snack area and private bath. There are some antique furnishings, as well as several reproductions. The attic suite has two full bathrooms and two bedrooms and is quite popular with larger families. In general, the painted walls in all the suites are hung with oil paintings, mirrors, and framed prints. In warmer months the two-level bricked courtyard, screened by a wall from the street, has a table and chairs set up for the guests' use. Breakfast is served at the McCampbell Inn across the street.

Accommodations: 1 room and 6 suites, all with private bath. *Pets:* Not permitted. *Driving Instructions:* Take I-81 to the Lexington exit. The inn is at the corner of Main and Washington streets.

THE McCAMPBELL INN

11 North Main Street, Lexington, VA 24450. 703-463-2044. *Innkeeper:* Don Fredenburg. Open all year.

The McCampbell Inn was built as a town house for John McCampbell and his family in 1809, and two new wings were added over the next fifty years. The building served as the town's telephone office and post office for a while. In 1982 the Peter Meredith family bought and restored the McCampbell house and the Alexander-Withrow House across the street. Don Fredenburg manages them both under the title Historic Country Inns of Lexington. The McCampbell Inn was decorated and furnished with period antiques. Although the inn provides visitors with lodgings in keeping with the historic character of Lexington, the rooms are equipped with modern heating, air conditioning, and baths, as well as telephones and refreshment bars with hot pots, coffee, tea, and juice. Breakfast is served in the Great Room downstairs. The inn is in the center of town, with many restaurants nearby.

Accommodations: 14 rooms and 2 suites, all with private bath. *Pets:* Not permitted. *Driving Instructions:* Take I-81 to the Lexington exit. The inn is at the corner of Main and Washington streets.

Mathews, Virginia

RIVERFRONT HOUSE

Route 14 East, Mathews, Virginia. Mailing address: P.O. Box 310, Mathews, VA 23109. 804-725-9975. *Innkeeper:* Annette Waldman Goldreyer. Open April to November.

Years ago, daffodils were a major crop in this town, and they still spring up wild each April. True to its name, Riverfront House stands at the edge of Put In Creek, near the mouth of the East River. This 1840 farmhouse, with its wraparound veranda, is less than an hour's drive from Williamsburg and Busch Gardens but is a world away from the more commercial attractions of that area.

Inside, the inn has a gracious entrance hall and staircase, mahogany mantels in the living room, and lace curtains in the dining room. Colorful scatter rugs decorate the bedrooms, of which all but one are air-conditioned. In the exception, a ceiling fan provides breezes on the few occasions they are needed. A breakfast buffet of fresh fruits, cheeses, breads, and muffins is served in the dining room.

Mathews is a sleepy village which dates from Revolutionary times. Today most residents either fish, crab, or farm for a living. There are several small shops in town, Chesapeake Bay is a ten-minute drive away, and two riverfront seafood restaurants are within five miles.

Accommodations: 5 rooms with shared bath. *Pets:* Not permitted. *Driving Instructions:* Take Route 17 south through Saluda to Glenns. Then take Route 198 to Mathews and continue east for ½ mile. The inn is the third driveway past the bus shelter, on the right.

Middleburg is in the heart of Virginia's hunt country with rolling hills and country fields neatly bounded by age-old fieldstone walls. It is an area of great beauty and half-hidden horse farms and estates. The picture-postcard town is only 25 miles from Dulles Airport and 50 miles from the nation's capital. Middleburg consists of historic old brick and native-stone buildings housing little shops and eateries. The *Middleburg Antiques Center*, one block west of the Red Fox Tavern, is in a three-story restored old home. Here, twenty antiques dealers sell a wide range of pieces.

THE RED FOX INN & TAVERN AND STRAY FOX INN

East Washington, Middleburg, VA 22117. 703-687-6301. *Innkeepers:* Turner and Dana Reuter. Open all year.

The Red Fox Tavern, everything an eighteenth-century inn should be, got off to an auspicious start. In 1731, the land was surveyed by a lad of only sixteen—George Washington. A tavern had been located on the spot for three years, so the future president probably paused for refreshment before continuing his task. In time, the tavern came to be called Chinn's Ordinary, and by 1812, it had grown to thirty-five rooms with an extensive wine cellar. Called The Beveridge House for the next sixty-five years, the inn provided a meeting place for the Confederate General J. E. B. Stuart. In the midst of fierce fighting, he and Colonel John Mosby met there to plan their offensives, and a room today bears Mosby's name.

The 30-inch stone walls of the Red Fox Tavern remain unscathed by time. After it was bought by Nancy Reuter in 1976, it received an exacting restoration. Extensive work was done to duplicate period wallpapers and to choose paint colors appropriate to the inn's eighteenth-century heritage. Each of the inn's many mantels (six of the fireplaces are in guest rooms) were carefully stripped of layers of paint and redone. Each mantel is different; the one in the Mosby room is particularly distinctive, with a tall, six-paneled front. The guest-room fireplaces and those in the public rooms are in full working order.

The main dining room (one of seven) is characterized by heavy, 16-inch-square posts that are hung with copper pots and support the dark-beamed ceiling. Windsor chairs, tavern tables, and hunt memo-

rabilia and sporting prints set the mood. Country breakfasts, lunches, and dinners are available to guests and the public. The wine list includes selections from nearby vineyards.

The Red Fox Tavern's guest rooms are decorated and furnished with period antiques. Most of the four-poster beds have canopies, and several rooms have their original fireplaces. Fresh flowers, bedside sweets, private phones, and thick cotton robes are thoughtful extra touches. The Stray Fox Inn is the annex and a recent acquisition. Built before the Civil War, it served as an inn and tavern for travelers on the stagecoach run on the old Alexandria-Winchester Turnpike. There are stenciled floors and walls, hooked rugs, and period antiques. The former stable now houses a specialty shop, and the old smoke house is an art gallery specializing in sporting prints.

Accommodations: 12 rooms with private bath. *Pets:* Not permitted. *Driving Instructions:* Take I-66 to Route 50, which leads directly to Middleburg and the inn.

WELBOURNE

Route 743, Middleburg, VA 22117. 703-687-3201. *Innkeeper:* Mrs.
N. H. Morison. Open all year.

For almost a century and a half, Middleburg has been the undisputed
center of fox hunting in America. The local hunt was founded in 1840
by Colonel Dulany, who also founded the country's oldest horse
show, the Upperville Colt and Horse Show. Colonel Dulany lived in
the family mansion known as Welbourne and was the great-grand-
father of the current innkeeper's husband. In all, seven generations of
the same family have occupied this superb old Virginia home; now,
each year, privileged travelers may also stay here.

Welbourne was built in sections, beginning with a stone house constructed in 1775, with additions from 1820 through 1870. The mansion retains seven generations of family heirlooms in an especially Southern and refined atmosphere. Welbourne continues to be a working farm, and its rural location assures a tranquil stay. Five of the inn's guest rooms have working fireplaces, although a modest fee is charged for the firewood. In addition to the rooms within the mansion, there are two cottages on the grounds, each of which can sleep four. Each morning, guests are treated to a hearty Southern breakfast of sausage, grits, eggs, fried tomatoes or apples, and so on, served at the mansion's dining-room table.

One must assume that these meals are considerably more relaxed than the one enjoyed by General Jeb Stuart, who, it is reported, ate his morning meal at Welbourne on horseback in front of the porch as bullets ticked off the building's tin roof. In the 1920s, Scribner's editor Maxwell Perkins was a frequent visitor and often sent his more promising authors to Middleburg for relaxation. Thomas Wolfe and F. Scott Fitzgerald were among the prominent guests. Fitzgerald wrote that he was "fascinated with the quality of that place."

Accommodations: 7 rooms with private bath, plus 4 cottages. *Driving Instructions:* From the center of Middleburg, take Route 50 3½ miles west to Route 611; turn right and go 1½ miles to Route 743. Turn left and drive 1.2 miles to the inn, on your left.

Middletown, Virginia

WAYSIDE INN SINCE 1797

7783 Main Street, Middletown, VA 22645. 703-869-1797. *Innkeeper:* Charles Alverson III. Open all year.

For many years one of our favorite country inns has been the Wayside Inn in Sudbury, Massachusetts. Another of our favorites, below the Mason-Dixon line, bears the same name. The Wayside Inn in Middletown has been offering fine food and lodgings since 1797. In its early days it was a way-station on the heavily traveled Shenandoah Valley Turnpike, offering food, lodging, and teams of fresh horses to arriving coaches. During the Civil War the inn was called the Wilkenson's Tavern and alternately served soldiers from both the North and the South. Because of the inn's established history of hospitality, it became one of America's first motor inns when the horseless carriage replaced coaches and buggies. In 1905, two wings were added onto the already substantial brick main building. The inn continued its tradition of service in its original state until 1961, when it was purchased by a Washington financier and realtor who began its restoration.

Today, the Wayside Inn has room after room of fine antiques that are in use and not merely on display. Eight of its rooms are devoted to dining, and they range in décor from elegantly formal colonial style to the rough-bricked simplicity of the former slave quarters. The latter, a favorite with many travelers who enjoy its crackling winter fire, was hidden for many years and was discovered fairly recently and restored to its present state. It had originally housed the slaves who waited there for the arrival of coaches in the early days of the inn. Meals start with a choice of several appetizers, of which Virginia peanut soup is the Southern specialty. Entrées include country ham and red-eye gravy, prime ribs of beef, pan-fried chicken, and roast pork. There are several steak and seafood selections for those who prefer them. Among the favorite desserts are pecan pie and carrot cake. The inn also serves breakfast and luncheon, and its waitresses wear colonial costumes, adding to the early-American atmosphere.

Many of the guest accommodations at the Wayside have canopied beds and working fireplaces, and many are decorated in Chinese, Victorian, and Empire styles.

Accommodations: 12 rooms and 9 suites with private bath. *Pets:* Not permitted. *Driving Instructions:* The inn is on Route 11, ½ mile south of exit 77 on I-81.

Monterey, Virginia

HIGHLAND INN

Main Street, Monterey, Virginia. Mailing address: P.O. Box 40, Monterey, VA 24465. 703-468-2143. *Innkeeper:* Bob Campbell. Open all year.

The restoration of this historic old mountain resort, once known as the Monterey Hotel, won back its former reputation as "The Pride of the Mountains" and earned it a place in the National Register of Historic Places.

The Highland Inn, built in 1904, is a white clapboard structure dominating the main street of this hamlet. Two stories of gingerbreaded porches stretch across its facade. The Saunderses refurbished some of the hotel's original old iron bedsteads and scoured the countryside for Victorian and Edwardian antiques to decorate the rooms. Colorful quilts brighten the beds, and country curtains decorate the windows. Halls are softly lighted by brass lamps with green glass shades. The ground floor's small, airy dining room serves three meals a day, with specialties of local trout and Virginia ham. The Black Sheep Tavern was recently added to the back of the hotel, and a small gift shop sells local crafts here. The inn's old-fashioned parlor is a popular gathering spot for guests. The Highland Inn is in a historic district surrounded by more than 3 million acres of national forest.

Accommodations: 20 rooms with private bath. *Driving Instructions:* From Staunton, Virginia, take Route 250 west for 45 miles.

Orange, Virginia

MAYHURST INN

Route 15 South, Orange, Virginia. Mailing address: P.O. Box 707, Orange, VA 22960. 703-672-5597. *Innkeepers:* Stephen and Shirley Ramsey. Open all year.

The Mayhurst Inn is a fanciful Italianate Victorian mansion on 36 acres of magnolias, towering oaks, and Osage orange trees, overlooking meadows with grazing cows, a farm pond, and the distant town of Orange. The mansion was built in 1859 by Colonel John Willis, great-nephew of President James Madison. Willis reportedly bought the land from Dolly Madison to help relieve her financial burdens. The house is now listed in the National Register of Historic Places.

Inside, a magnificent oval staircase ascends four floors to a roof-top gazebo. The Ramseys have furnished the rooms with a large collection of antiques, the overflow being offered for sale in their antique shop in the barn. Guest rooms, many with Palladian windows, balconies, and wallpaper, have wonderful beds, some high enough to require steps. A ground-floor guest room has its own patio, and both the room and patio are decorated with mountain twig furniture. There are three sitting rooms. Breakfast and afternoon tea are served in the dining room.

Accommodations: 7 rooms, 6 with private bath. *Driving Instructions:* From Charlottesville, take I-64 to Zions Crossroads and then follow Route 15 north. The inn is ¼ mile south of Orange on Rt. 15.

Richmond, Virginia

THE CATLIN-ABBOTT HOUSE

2304 East Broad Street, Richmond, VA 23223. 804-780-3746. *Innkeeper:* Frances L. Abbott. Open all year.

The Catlin-Abbott House has a distinguished history. Built in 1845, its superb brick masonry is the mark of master craftsman William Mitchell, who was William Catlin's slave. So skilled was Mitchell that Catlin frequently hired him out to other Richmond families to build their homes. Mitchell's daughter, Maggie Walker, grew up to become this country's first woman bank president.

The Catlins lived in their house only a few years before moving a few doors away. Following the Civil War, a six-room extension was added to the house at 2304 Broad Street to accommodate boarders, a common post-war practice. It is these rooms which now house quarters for Dr. and Mrs. Abbott and the spacious original bedrooms available for overnight guests. Everywhere one looks, the dignity of a fine Southern home is evident: Oriental rugs, Czechoslovakian crystal chandeliers, lace-trimmed four-poster beds, working fireplaces in most guest rooms, mahogany tables and chairs, and polished pine floors. From the inn's veranda, one can look out over the garden, which blooms almost continuously from March through November. In the morning, one may choose to have breakfast in bed or in the dining room. In either case, the meal is served on Lenox china, with sterling silver flatware. After breakfast, most guests make their first sightseeing stop at St. John's church, just a block away. It was here that Patrick Henry uttered the words, "Give me liberty or give me death."

Accommodations: 4 rooms, 3 with private bath, and a 2-bedroom suite. *Pets and children:* Not permitted. *Driving Instructions:* From I-95 northbound, take Exit 10 to the first traffic light (Broad Street), turn left and proceed east to the 2300 block.

THE CONYERS HOUSE

Slate Mills Road, Sperryville, VA 22740. 703-987-8025. *Innkeepers:* Norman and Sandra Cartwright-Brown. Open all year.

The Conyers House is located, according to one of the local folks, "right there on Kilby's Creek at the foot of Walden Mountain by that ol' cottonwood tree. If you go by Dick Jenkin's white chickens, you done gone too far." After beginning as a store around 1770, acquiring an addition in 1810, and passing almost 200 years as, in turn, a tollhouse, post office, and country store, the rambling, four-story frame building was restored in 1979 and transformed into an appealing country inn. The innkeepers are two lively world travelers who speak French, Italian, German, and a little Arabic and treat their guests like dear old friends. Sandra rides with the Rappahannock hunt and encourages all visitors to enjoy a trailride through the Blue Ridge scenery.

The inn is furnished throughout with an eclectic blend of antiques and family treasures gathered from around the world. All are set off by the old stone fireplaces and low-beamed ceilings of the rooms. Sandra Cartwright-Brown is quick to weed out the faint of heart on the

phone with accurate descriptions of the lack of certain modern amenities at the inn, such as central heating in several of the rooms. To stay here is to be whisked back to the eighteenth century, with its symphony of crackling fires, creaking stairs, and century-old floors, and winds rattling across the old tin roof. Breakfast is a gourmet affair; with advance notice, dinner is served to guests. The Conyers House is just minutes from a *nouvelle* French restaurant, the Inn at Little Washington.

Accommodations: 8 rooms, 3 with private bath. *Pets and children:* Not permitted. *Driving Instructions:* Write for detailed instructions. Sperryville is west of Washington, D.C., near Skyline Drive in the Blue Ridge Mountains.

Stanley, Virginia

JORDAN HOLLOW FARM INN

Route 626, Stanley, Virginia. Mailing address: Route 2, P.O. Box 375, Staunton, VA 22851. 703-778-2209 or 778-2285. *Innkeepers:* Marley and Jetze Beers. Open all year.

Jordan Hollow Farm offers guests a chance to enjoy country-inn comfort in the surroundings of a working two-hundred-year-old horse farm on rolling meadows at the foot of the Blue Ridge Mountains and Shenandoah National Park. The inn's oldest part, the restaurant, is housed within two log cabins built in 1790, with rooms added over the years. The "new" part of the house was completed in 1882, and an old lodge, horse barn, and hay barn are about the same age. Rowe's Lodge was designed to match the farmhouse in style.

Innkeeper Jetze Beers is Dutch and moved to this country only a few years ago; he loves to entertain guests with anecdotes from his homeland. Marley is an artist and horsewoman, and she often can be found training the Holsteiner horses she raises for show jumping.

Public rooms at Jordan Hollow include a rustic bar and lounge where beer and wines are served and where there are occasional country-music evenings. The dining room offers all three meals to guests and the public. The dinner menu includes rib-eye steak, sautéed trout, quail, pork chops, ham, and broiled chicken breast.

Accommodations: 20 rooms with private bath. *Pets:* Not permitted, but boarding kennels are nearby. *Driving Instructions:* Take Route 340, which is 6 miles south of Lauray, turn left on Route 624, right on Route 689, and left on Route 626.

FREDERICK HOUSE

New and Frederick streets, Staunton, Virginia. Mailing address: P.O. Box 1387, Staunton, VA 24401. 703-885-4220. *Innkeepers:* Joe and Evy Harmon. Open all year.

Staunton is a historic Virginia town in central Shenandoah Valley, not far from Skyline Drive and the Blue Ridge Parkway. Its many early homes and businesses have benefited from the preservationist spirit pervading the area. Staunton is also the home of Mary Baldwin College and the Woodrow Wilson Birthplace.

Frederick House is actually three town houses built between 1810 and 1910, which have been restored and furnished with antiques, period pieces, and comfortable upholstered chairs and sofas. The brick buildings, which have classic lines and a balustered portico, have been painted a soft gray with white trim. Within, eleven rooms and suites have carpeted floors, colorful wallpapers, air-conditioning, and television. A Continental breakfast is served in guests' rooms or suites. Next door, an athletic club offers indoor swimming, and tennis is nearby. The Harmons, who are familiar with the area, can direct guests to the many local activities.

Accommodations: 11 rooms and suites with private bath. *Pets and smoking:* Not permitted. *Driving Instructions:* Take either I-81 or I-64 to Staunton. In downtown Staunton, Frederick Street is a block north of Beverly Street. The inn is at the corner of Frederick and New streets.

Strasburg, Virginia

HOTEL STRASBURG

201 Holiday Street, Strasburg, VA 22657. 703-465-9191. *Innkeeper*: Michael Paper. Open all year.

The historic Hotel Strasburg has stood for nearly a century at the corner of Queen and Holiday streets in the town of Strasburg. The large, white Victorian building is a classic example of American turn-of-the-century architecture. Originally built as a hospital by a Dr. Bruin in the early nineteenth century, it has undergone many restorations and remodelings. An adjacent house was moved from its corner position so the hospital could be built. The large building to the southwest was the carriage house and is now apartments. Dr. Bruin's residence still stands just three houses from the hotel. In 1910, after Dr. Bruin's death, the hospital was sold and transformed into a hotel. The

Wayside World Corp. bought the hotel in 1976 and began extensive restoration and remodeling. It is now furnished with many antiques, prints, and British memorabilia. The parlor-lobby contains potted ferns, an old organ, and velvet side chairs. The spacious halls outside the guest rooms and suites are furnished with groupings of antique chairs, love seats, and marble-topped commodes. The guest rooms are bright and sunny with flowered wallpapers, marble-topped bureaus, and large antique beds—some of scrolly iron, others of heavy dark woods carved in a Victorian style. These rooms are furnished with conversation pieces out of the hotel's past. The private bathrooms contain such period fixtures as vintage tubs and showers, and each room has individually controlled heating and air conditioning.

The hotel and its pub were designed to convey the atmosphere of an old English country inn. The Queen Victoria and Lord Nelson dining rooms serve American and British fare to guests of the hotel and the public.

Strasburg, in the heart of the Shenandoah Valley, is of much historic significance. It was strategic to both North and South in the Civil War. The *Strasburg Museum,* housed in the old Southern Railway depot, exhibits authentic eighteenth- and nineteenth-century articles as they were used, a collection of the small-town memorabilia, and an outstanding display of Indian artifacts. Area residents work with professional actors to put on a passion play each evening from late June to Labor Day. It is performed under the stars in the natural amphitheater on the grounds of one of the old Strasburg homes. The *Strasburg Emporium,* at 306 East King Street, offers numerous booths with all sorts of collectibles and foodstuffs. It is in the remodeled old Strasburg Textile Company.

Accommodations: 19 rooms, 6 with private bath. *Driving Instructions:* The hotel is in a residential district of Strasburg. Take exit 76 off I-81. Strasburg is on Route 11, and the hotel is at the corner of Queen and Holiday streets.

Trevilians, Virginia

Trevilians, a quiet area east of Charlottesville, is just remote enough to make enjoying the countryside the most important "activity" in these parts. Within driving distance is *Monticello*, the home of Thomas Jefferson and *Ash Lawn*, the home of James Monroe. Also nearby are the home of James and Dolly Madison and the birthplace of George Clark of the Lewis and Clark expeditions.

INN AT PROSPECT HILL
Route 613 near Zion Crossroads, Virginia. Mailing address: R.D. 1, Box 55, Trevilians, VA 23170. 703-967-0844. *Innkeepers*: Bill and Mireille Sheehan. Open all year except Christmas.

Prospect Hill lives up to what most people expect in a small, romantic Southern country inn. The original building dates from 1732, with additions as late as 1880. It is an intact example of a working Virginia plantation with its original outbuildings. Guest rooms have been created in the manor house and the slave quarters. Guests arriving for dinner are encouraged to stroll around the grounds or sit on the veranda getting acquainted. In the cooler weather, they frequently gather in the foyer and parlor and enjoy the fire in the fireplace. No menu is posted at the inn, and there is but one seating. After a blessing by innkeeper Bill Sheehan, a four-course dinner is served, with the selections changing daily. Beer and wine are available with dinner, which is served Wednesday through Saturday only. Overnight guests are served a full breakfast in bed when they awaken (any time after 8 A.M.). Surrounded by 40 acres of property, the inn affords opportunities for hiking through woods and pastureland.

Rooms at the inn are furnished with some antiques and feature such touches as quilt-covered four-posters, and fireplaces in six of the seven rooms. The Sheehans go out of their way to make their guests feel at home. Although dinner is available to the general public, the real fun of a trip to the inn is staying in one of the attractive guest rooms.

Accommodations: 7 rooms with private bath. *Pets:* Not permitted. *Driving Instructions:* From Charlottesville, take Route 250 east 1 mile past Zion Crossroads. Take a left (north) on Route 613 and drive 3 miles to the inn. From Washington, D.C., go west on Route 66 to Warrenton, then take Route 29 south to Culpepper. Take Route 15 south to Gordonsville, then Route 33 east 8 miles to the stop sign. Turn left at the stop sign and go 100 feet, then turn right onto Route 613 and drive 7 miles to the inn.

Upperville, Virginia

GIBSON HALL INN

Route 50, Upperville, Virginia. Mailing address: Box 225, Upperville, VA 22176. 703-592-3514. *Innkeeper:* Carol Beecher. Open all year.

Upperville is an historic town in the heart of Virginia's hunt country, which has all manner of horse-related activities, such as stable tours, horse shows, and races. The area is surrounded by the Blue Ridge Mountains and is located just an hour from Washington, D.C.

Gibson Hall was built in 1832 by the Gibson family and owned by their descendants until 1983, when the estate was purchased and meticulously renovated as a bed-and-breakfast inn. The building retains its fine Federal- and Greek Revival-style architectural features. Oriental rugs are set on polished pine floors, the original chandeliers have been electrified, and marble fireplaces are a reminder of an elegant earlier era. The inn's public rooms are simply furnished with antiques and tasteful reproductions of upholstered period pieces such as wing chairs and loveseats. In the evening, Carol provides guests with an opportunity to get to know each other over complimentary Virginia wines and cheese, served by the fire in the formal dining room. Here a Continental breakfast is also served. The guest rooms have either brass or four-poster beds; all but one have fireplaces.

Accommodations: 6 rooms, 4 with private bath. *Pets and small children:* Not permitted. *Driving Instructions:* The inn is on Route 50 West, 10 miles from Middleburg.

Vesuvius, Virginia

SUGAR TREE LODGE

Highway 56, Vesuvius, VA 24483. 703-377-2197. *Innkeeper:* Dean
Gregory. Open April through November.

Sugar Tree Lodge is a rustic country inn on the side of a mountain
some 3000 feet up in Virginia's Blue Ridge Mountains. From the
porch rockers, one can see 27 miles down the Shenandoah Valley or
across to neighboring mountain meadows. The ride to the inn is an
adventure in itself: a three-mile drive straight up the mountain, culmi-
nating in a hairpin turn down the gravel lane and across a log bridge
spanning a rushing mountain stream. Here, tucked into the terraced
mountainside are the lodge, a gate house, and a guest house, each
assembled in pioneer mountain traditions from several late eigh-
teenth- and early-nineteenth-century Virginia log structures.

Inside the lodge are several antique-filled guest rooms, a dining
room, a tavern, a solarium-greenhouse, and a terraced dining area
facing right into the mountain, rising straight up. The rooms are furnished with Shenandoah antiques from the early nineteenth century,
plus later oak and chestnut pieces. The lounge has comfortable soft
leather couches grouped in front of a stone hearth and chimney, complete with a moosehead above the mantle.

Upstairs, a private dining room has a log balcony overlooking the
living room. There is a well-stocked library on the landing, presided
over by a stuffed wild turkey in full Thanksgiving regalia. Each guest
room has its own fireplace and modern bath, along with antiques,
quilts, and chinked log or barnsided walls. Fresh flowers and a complimentary bottle of Virginia wine are welcoming touches.

The dining rooms are open to guests for breakfast and to the public for lunch and dinner. The blackboard menu offers French nouvelle
cuisine using fresh local ingredients. The word is out and the restaurant is packed on weekends; reservations are a must.

The mountain offers recreation or peaceful solitude, depending on
guests' desires. There are a swimming hole down the hill and a
20,000-acre game preserve. One hiking trail leads to a waterfall.

Accommodations: 10 rooms, 8 with private bath. *Pets:* Not permitted. *Children:* Not encouraged. *Driving Instructions:* Take Route
11 about 17 miles north of Lexington to Steele's Tavern. Turn east on
Route 56. The lodge is 2.8 miles past the village of Vesuvius.

Warm Springs, Virginia

THE INN AT GRISTMILL SQUARE

Gristmill Square, P.O. Box 359, Warm Springs, VA 24484. 703-839-2311. *Innkeepers*: Jack and Janice McWilliams. Open all year except early March.

Gristmill Square is a restoration of an old gristmill and its companion buildings. The Warm Springs Run was described by Thomas Jefferson in 1781 as "a very bold stream, sufficient to work a gristmill." There has been a mill on this creek since 1771, but the present buildings were constructed near the end of the nineteenth century. Gristmill Square looks very much like a Williamsburg restoration, with lovely color combinations, trim brick sidings, manicured paths, and landscaping. The inn at Gristmill Square includes the inn and the Waterwheel Restaurant, a country store, and an art gallery.

The guest rooms at the inn are airy and spacious, and some have wood-burning fireplaces. Rooms are partially furnished with antiques. Each has its own sitting area, telephone, bath, and color television set. The Board Room, a corner hideaway, is filled with nineteenth-century rough-dressed American chestnut boards, some as wide as 18 inches. The Dinwiddie Room boasts a carved eighteenth-century mantel of dark pine and poplar from a nearby historic site. The Silo Suite has a round room leading to a rectangular bedroom and modern furnishings and decor. The Tower Apartment is a complete, two-bedroom unit with kitchen and sun deck in a Victorian-style turret. The Main Street Apartment has a balcony with a view of the lovely Victorian town and nearby mountains.

The Waterwheel Restaurant is part of the old gristmill with its revolving overshoot waterwheel. The main dining room has the old millstones still in their housings, most of the original locust flooring, exposed beams, rough siding, and the slender grain chutes. The furnishings blend right in; there are worn rush-seat, ladder-back chairs with calico and gingham-checked cushions, and fresh flowers on the little square tables. Guests are provided with Continental breakfasts; the restaurant is open to the public and guests for lunch and dinner, except on Mondays. The specialty of the house is rainbow trout, brought in daily. The menu includes homemade soups and veal dishes. The wine cave is located amid the wheels and gears of the mill, and guests are welcome to explore the machinery and select their own wine. The Simon Kenton Pub fitted into the miller's office has dark green walls, old prints and memorabilia, and old-fashioned tavern stools, and can accommodate about ten patrons. It was named for a famous frontiersman who was a friend of Daniel Boone. Guests at the inn are entitled to use the inn's bath and tennis club just across the way, which offers tennis, saunas, and a swimming pool.

Accommodations: 14 rooms with private bath. *Driving Instructions:* All routes to Warm Springs are scenic treats. From Lexington on I-81, take Route 39 west to Warm Springs. From Roanoke, take Route 220. From Staunton, Virginia, on I-81, take Route 254 to Buffalo Gap, Route 42 to Millboro Springs, then Route 39 to Warm Springs. The inn is at the junction with Route 645.

MEADOW LANE LODGE

Route 39, Warm Springs, Virginia. Mailing address: Star Route A, Box 110, Warm Springs, VA 24484. 703-839-5959. *Innkeepers:* Philip and Catherine Hirsh. Open April through January.

In the heart of the Virginia Allegheny Mountains lie Warm Springs and the Hirshes' 1,600 acres of woods, fields, and streams. The area is picture-postcard perfect in all seasons, and the Meadow Lane Lodge is a natural part of that scene, its pastoral setting, its lawn and bordering trim hedges, and its many varieties of wildflowers and birds providing an ideal home-base for nature lovers of all kinds. Two miles of the Jackson River meander through the estate, and the Hirshes keep it well stocked with trout for fly-casting enthusiasts at the lodge.

Meadow Lane blends contemporary comfort and furnishings with antique pieces. The spacious living room has a pair of stone fireplaces with fires going on chilly mornings and evenings. A full country breakfast is served from a 1710 sideboard in the sunny porch–dining room. It is the only meal served, although the Hirshes will help guests with dinner reservations at any of the excellent restaurants in the area.

Meadow Lane Lodge accepts no more than sixteen guests at a time, making the stay, for most, seem like a house party. The guest rooms vary from spacious doubles to suites with living rooms and fireplaces to a choice of private antique-filled cottages. Craig's Cottage is on the Meadow Lane estate and has its own fireplace. Francisco Cottage is on the steep hillside above Gristmill Square, in the village itself. A particular favorite of ours, it has a full living room with brick fireplace and kitchen, a porch with a view of the surrounding hillside, and a comfortably furnished bedroom.

Accommodations: 8 rooms with private bath. *Pets:* Not permitted. *Driving Instructions:* All routes to Warm Springs are scenic treats. From Lexington on I-81, then Route 39 west to Warm Springs. From Roanoke, take Route 220. From Staunton, Viginia, on I-81, take Route 254 to Buffalo Gap, Route 42 to Millboro Springs, then Route 39 to Warm Springs. The lodge entrance is 4 miles west of Warm Springs on Route 39.

Warm Springs is nestled in a beautiful valley in the Alleghenies; some of the valley rock formations are thought by geologists to be the oldest known. In Warm Springs Valley there is a rim of Ordovician older than the carbon beds where coal is found. The peaceful Victorian hamlet has churches and a cemetery dating from the 1800s, and the old ham house where Virginia hams once were processed. On Courthouse Square is an old law-office building that houses the Bath County Historical Society and its interesting collections of Indian artifacts and local families' heirlooms. It is open Friday and Saturday from 3 to 5, June through October. Gristmill Square is a restoration of old buildings that contains shops and a gallery showing local artists' works.

The actual Warm Springs bubbles up some 1,200 gallons of crystal-clear 96.5° water per minute. It has been a health spa since the Indian and colonial times.

Williamsburg, Virginia

WILLIAMSBURG INN AND COLONIAL HOUSES

South Francis Street, Williamsburg, Virginia. Mailing address:
P.O. Drawer B, Williamsburg, VA 23185. 804-229-1000. *Innkeeper:* Bruce P. Hearn. Open all year.

The Williamsburg Inn, with its 232 rooms, is not strictly a country
inn, but it is one of the country's finest and most attentive small
hotels. It opened in 1937 as part of the Rockefeller plan for
Williamsburg's development, and it bears his penchant for perfection.
Largely furnished in the Regency manner, it has thick carpeting,

formal settings, swagged draperies, and chandeliers. Distinguished visitors at the inn have included many presidents and other heads of state, as well as royalty. Some of the more formal meals in the Williamsburg Inn are served in the Regency dining room. Here the fading tradition of coats and ties for gentlemen is still upheld, though it has eased a bit for women, who are now admitted in pants suits. The inn offers the most elaborate overnight accommodations in the village, with many large suites available in both the original inn and its more recent guest wings, known as Providence Hall. A number of the suites in these modern buildings have fireplaces and private terraces overlooking the nearby golf courses and tennis courts.

The charm of a Williamsburg visit is enhanced by the many Colonial Houses that provide lodging within the historic village, with full hotel services provided by the Williamsburg Inn. Here, a country-inn atmosphere prevails. There are sixteen rooms in the dormered Brick House Tavern, and many rooms are tucked into converted colonial kitchens complete with the original fireplaces. Others still are in former shops that now provide overnight comfort for twentieth-century guests. At one time, the colonial laundry served the townhouse of an owner of a great plantation, who was a member of the Governor's Council. The laundry is now a one-room cottage in its own secluded garden. The Chiswell House is a white clapboard building reminiscent of a Virginia plantation home; the Market Square Tavern has survived from the early days of Williamsburg and now offers thirteen guest rooms and its restored living rooms. The furnishings of the Colonial Houses are in keeping with their period, with plenty of canopied beds as well as the modern convenience of air conditioning. These are by no means the only accommodations offered by Colonial Williamsburg. Others tend to be more motel-like but still maintain the high standard established by John D. Rockefeller, Jr., more than fifty years ago. There is a complete list of motels and guest houses in the area, and Colonial Williamsburg will be happy to steer you to alternatives.

Accommodations: 232 rooms with private bath, plus various accommodations in restored colonial houses. *Driving Instructions:* Take I-64 to Williamsburg. Follow the green information signs to the Colonial Williamsburg Information Center, where instructions to the inn or Colonial houses will be given.

Index of Inns

WITH ROOM-RATE AND CREDIT-CARD INFORMATION

Index of Inns

Inns are listed in the chart that follows. In general, rates given are for two persons unless otherwise stated. Single travelers should inquire about special rates. The following abbreviations are used throughout the chart:

dbl. =   double. These rates are for two persons in a room.
dbl. oc. =   double occupancy. These rates depend on two persons being registered for the room. Rentals of the room by a single guest will usually involve a different rate basis.
EP =   European Plan: no meals.
MAP =   Modified American Plan: rates include dinner and breakfast. Readers should confirm if stated rates are per person or per couple.
AP =   American Plan: rates include all meals. Readers should confirm if stated rates are per person or per couple.
BB =   Bed and Breakfast: rates include full or Continental breakfast.

Credit-Card Abbreviations

AE =   American Express   MC =   MasterCard
CB =   Carte Blanche   V =   Visa
DC =   Diners Club

Important: All rates are the most recent available but are subject to change. Check with the inn before making reservations.

Boone Tavern Hotel, 77; rates: $28 to $40 dbl. EP; AE, MC, V

Buckhorn Inn, 193; rates: $78 dbl. MAP, cottages $90

Burn, 105; rates: $75 dbl. BB; MC, V

Casa de Solana, 30; rates: $50 to $75 per room BB; AE, MC, V

Castle, The, 222; rates: $50 dbl. BB

Catlin-Abbott House, 259; rates: $60 to $75 dbl. BB; AE, MC, V

Chalet Suzanne Inn and Restaurant, 28; rates: $50 to $80 dbl. EP; AE, CB, DC, MC, V

Channel Bass Inn, 238; rates: $80 to $150 dbl. EP; AE, DC, MC, V

Clewiston Inn, 26; rates: $40 dbl. EP; AE, CB, DC, MC, V

Colonel Ludlow House, 177; rates: $55 to $90 dbl. BB; AE, MC, V

Colonial Inn, 155; rates: $35 to $40 dbl. EP; AE, MC, V

Conyers House, 260; rates: $80 to $100 dbl. BB

Corbett House, 140; rates: $35 to $35 dbl. BB; AE, MC, V

Cottage Plantation, 101; rates: $60 dbl. BB

Country Place Hotel, 210; rates: $25 to $30 dbl. EP

Crescent Cottage Inn, 9; rates: $40 dbl. BB

Crescent Hotel, 10; rates: $45 to $55 dbl. EP; AE, MC, V

Culpepper House, 73; rates: $36 dbl. BB

Dairy Hollow House, 12; rates: $59 dbl. BB; AE, MC, V

De Loffre House, 44; rates: $52 to $60 dbl. BB; AE, MC, V

Doe Run Inn, 79; rates: $37 dbl. EP; MC, V

Donoho Hotel, 197; rates: $50 dbl. AP

Driskill Hotel, 201; rates: $94 to $168 dbl. EP; AE, DC, MC, V

Edwardian Inn, 16; rates: $39 to $45 dbl. BB; AE, MC, V

1842 Inn, 55; rates: $55 to $85 dbl. BB; AE, MC, V

Eliza Thompson House, 65; rates: $78 to $98 dbl. BB; AE, MC, V

Elliott House Inn, 183; rates on request; AE, MC, V

Eseeola Lodge, 157; rates: $140 dbl. MAP; MC, V

Esmeralda Inn, 141; rates: $27 to $50 dbl. BB; MC, V

Excelsior House, 216; rates: $25 to $50 dbl. EP

Farris 1912, 207; rates: $35 to $50 dbl. EP except for hunting season, when AP rates apply; AE, MC, V

Faust Hotel, 223; rates: $35 and up dbl. EP; AE, CB, DC, MC, V

Fleur de Lis Inn, 87; rates: $55 dbl. BB; AE, MC, V

Flint Street Inn, 117; rates: $50 dbl. BB; AE, MC, V

Foley House Inn, 66; rates: $75 to $170 dbl. BB; AE, MC, V

Folkestone Lodge, 130; rates: $48 dbl. BB; MC, V

Franklin Terrace, 149; rates: $34 to $38 dbl. BB; MC, V

Frederick House, 263; rates: $30 to $45 dbl. BB; AE, MC, V

French Quarter Maisonnettes, 91; rates: $36 to $48 dbl. EP

Fryemont Inn, 131; rates: $36 to $46 dbl. EP, $62 to $75 dbl. MAP; MC, V

Gibson Hall Inn, 269; rates: $70 to $115 dbl. BB

Glencoe Plantation, 103; rates: $60 to $85 dbl. BB; MC, V

Graystone Guest House, 175; rates: $75 to $85 dbl. BB; AE, MC, V